14.95

Hmong in America

Journey from a Secret War

Text by
Tim Pfaff

Funded in part by the
National Endowment for the Humanities

Chippewa Valley Museum Press

Cover design: Jeanne Nyre
Layout design: Susan McLeod

Project Development Team

Chippewa Valley Museum

Julie Johnson
Curator of Collections

Susan McLeod
Director

Jeanne Nyre
Designer

Tim Pfaff
Curator of Public Programs

Diane Schmidt
Senior Curator

Eau Claire Area Hmong Mutual Assistance Association

Chou Lee
Executive Director

Joyce Metzgar
Assistant Director

Deanna Smugala
Assistant Director

Kao Xiong
Translation Services

Smidchei Xiong
Project Coordinator

Houa Yang
Project Coordinator

Principal Project Consultants

Janet Gilmore, Ph.D.
Wisconsin Folk Museum

James Leary, Ph.D.
University of Wisconsin - Madison
Wisconsin Folk Museum

Charles Lee, Ph.D.
History Department
University of Wisconsin - La Crosse

Alfred W. McCoy, Ph.D.
History Department
University of Wisconsin - Madison

Yong Kay Moua
Community Advisor

Elizabeth Quinn Owen (Perkins)
Textile Specialist

Cliff Sloane
Ethnomusicologist

Melissa Ringheim Stoddart
Anthropologist
Science Museum of Minnesota

Library of Congress Catalog Card Number: 95-67766
Pfaff, Tim. *Hmong in America:*
Journey from a Secret War.
Includes notes, bibliographic references and index.

ISBN 0-9636191-3-6

Table of Contents

Starting over in Eau Claire, Wisconsin, *the Lee family poses on a hill overlooking downtown. Standing, left-right: Kia Lor, Tou Lee, Chao Lor and Yong Koua Lee; kneeling, Pao Lee; seated: Yee Lee, Cha Lee, Peng Lee, Yia Lee, August 1987. Photographer: Neal Menschel,* ©The Christian Science Monitor. *As a college student, Pao Lee translated oral history interviews for the documentation project conducted by the Chippewa Valley Museum and the Eau Claire Area Hmong Mutual Assistance Association.*

Preface

In 1994, U.S. President Bill Clinton's decision to lift the trade embargo of Vietnam renewed the debate over what is sometimes described as America's longest and most tragic war. On both sides of the political spectrum, the Vietnam War continues to spark divisive, impassioned arguments among scholars and lay people. What are the lessons of Vietnam? Was American policy inherently flawed? Was the failure in the field or lack of support at home? Such debates often carry ideological rhetoric which has continued to ring out long after battlefields have fallen silent. One side is painted as benign, the other, malevolent; one leader is labeled hero, another villain.

America's involvement in Laos, and as a consequence its alliance with the Hmong, has received far less attention, yet is written about and debated with no less conviction. From 1961 to 1975, the U.S. Central Intelligence Agency actively recruited Laotian highlanders to fight a "secret war" in Laos in direct violation of the 1962 Geneva Accords. Hmong soldiers blocked supplies headed for South Vietnam and served as the primary "anti-communist" force in Laos. The multi-million-dollar operation, unreported in the American press until 1969, wreaked havoc on the land and its people. When American forces withdrew from Southeast Asia in 1975, thousands fled to Thailand as refugees and subsequently resettled in the United States.

The Hmong will likely remain unknown to most Americans, yet their experience cuts to the core of American politics, touching upon issues which have been widely debated throughout U.S. history. Under what circumstances should American might be projected overseas? Is it legitimate for the U.S. government to conduct military operations in foreign countries without public knowledge and support? Is it the obligation of the United States to provide a safe haven for refugees/immigrants around the world, as the credo on the Statue of Liberty implies? What is the best way to structure public assistance, so that it empowers the needy to become self-sufficient without creating a permanent "welfare class?" Finally, is it desireable or even appropriate for arriving immigrants to practice and pass down their own cultural traditions? Does this enhance or threaten American culture?

Hmong in America is one outcome of an on-going documentation effort begun in 1991 as a cooperative project conducted by the Chippewa Valley Museum (CVM) and the Eau Claire Area Hmong Mutual Assistance Association (HMAA). The HMAA, an organization dedicated to helping Hmong refugees adjust in American society, was responding to the desire by many adults to preserve Hmong history and culture for their children. CVM has a broad mission to preserve the history of the Chippewa Valley and its people and to present their stories to the public.

Air America's support of Hmong refugees and soldiers *represented a vital ingredient in the U.S./Hmong war effort in northern Laos, August 1971. Photographer: John Everingham. Alfred W. McCoy.*

Who are the Hmong?
Where did they come from?
What brought them to the United States?
How are they doing here?

In Laos, we helped you fight the war. The Americans came to live with our leaders in our country .... We provided food .... If the Americans came to our house, whatever we ate we treated the Americans equally .... Sometimes you had problems, even if we didn't know how to speak your language, we pointed fingers or demonstrated, trying to show what we meant .... If we found an injured American soldier ... we ... carried the American to the base .... In some dangerous situations, we were willing to let ten Hmong soldiers die so that one of your leaders could live ....

We still remember all the good things you did for us such as using planes to drop rice for our people wherever we went so that we would not starve .... We considered Americans as our own brothers .... Now we have lost our own country .... Those who made it here, they have the opportunity for education and jobs .... We started a new life so that our children would have a better life.

Chia Koua Xiong
Eau Claire, November 5, 1992
Interviewer: Smidchei Xiong
Translator: Pao Lee

The Journey of Chia Koua Xiong

Chia Koua Xiong is a respected elder and influential member of the Xiong clan in the Hmong community currently settled at Eau Claire, Wisconsin. He came to West Central Wisconsin as a refugee from Thailand in 1989. Already in his sixties when he arrived, Chia Koua speaks little English and, like many older people, has had great difficulty making the adjustment to American life. A respected civilian leader in northern Laos, Chia Koua possesses skills which have not enabled him to support his family in this country. While he renders well-received advice to Hmong families in Eau Claire, his role has been limited by his unfamiliarity with American culture. Slight of build with a gentle demeanor, there is little about his physical

Chia Koua Xiong, Long Tieng, Laos, 1968. Chao Xiong.

presence which would distinguish him as a man of stature. Certainly, lacking the material wealth which is so often used in the United States as a yardstick of success, Chia Koua would be passed over by many without hesitation. To know something of his life, however, is to understand a great deal about Hmong history, and the powerful and tragic events which have brought Hmong families to the United States.

Chia Koua can recount stories passed on to him in childhood of ancestors living in southern China, of their great 19th century exodus across the Yellow River to Southeast Asia fleeing armed suppression. He can recall formative years farming with his family in the rugged mountains of northern Laos. There he learned to build houses, to grow highland rice, to forge axe blades and flintlocks, and to play the *qeej* ("kheng"), a musical instrument used to guide departed spirits at funeral ceremonies.

As a young man, Chia Koua fought with French guerillas against the Japanese occupation of Laos during World War II. After the war, he continued to aid the French attempting to regain control of Vietnam, Laos, and Cambodia, their former colonies. Not all Hmong allied with the French, just as later, not all Hmong would side with the Americans. As a result of his military service, Chia Koua became a *naiban*, or village leader, and gradually moved up the Laotian political hierarchy. In 1961 he was again enlisted for military duty, this time by emerging leader Vang Pao who had been recruited by the Americans to lead an anti-communist force among the Laotian Hmong in Xieng Khouang Province. Hmong villages surrounded the vast Plain of Jars, a strategic plateau sought after by both communist and anti-communist forces in the escalating battle for Southeast Asia. The conflict widened existing political divisions between Laotian ethnic groups and, once swept up in the larger ideological struggle between the United States and the Soviet Union, assumed horrific proportions far out of balance with the local situation.

Chia Koua fought for more than a decade. He was wounded many times, and lost many relatives and friends. He saw the land pock-marked by aerial bombardments, and booby-trapped by hidden land mines or unexploded shells. In 1975, when the Americans withdrew, Chia Koua witnessed the same sort of scattering of Hmong people that his grandparents had years earlier described. Thousands immediately fled across the Mekong River to refugee camps in Thailand. Thousands took to the hills where they either

Chia Koua Xiong (center) received a warm welcome from Nao Tou Xiong (left) and Moua Xiong (right) upon his arrival at the airport in Eau Claire, January 30, 1989. Photographer: John Lindrud, Eau Claire Leader-Telegram.

In October 1946, the naikong said that I was a brave, understanding young man, and had the ability to help our country. He asked me to be the naiban .... In 1950 I was appointed as the kaitong. I governed all the people in the surrounding areas. While I was on duty, my wife and my children took care of our visitors, providing them food and shelter. In 1960, the Hmong people and the Laotians, living in the surrounding areas, saw that I was an understanding person, so they wanted me to work in the city as a representative for our area. I worked in the city from 1961 through 1963 .... I was appointed naikong. I worked for both the Hmong and Laotians because very few Hmong people knew how to speak Laotian. As naikong, I governed about 40,000-50,000 people.

Chia Koua Xiong
Eau Claire, November 5, 1992
Interviewer: Smidchei Xiong
Translator: Pao Lee

continued armed resistance against the new communist government, or tried to exist outside its reach. Thousands returned to their former villages and began the difficult task of repair. Thousands did not survive.

Since 1975, the United States has accepted more than 110,000 Laotian highlanders as refugees, the vast majority Hmong. As startling as Chia Koua's journey might seem to Americans, his experiences are shared by nearly every Hmong adult. They arrived with the heavy baggage of war and flight. They have struggled in this country to adjust to a landscape and society radically different from their own. In Eau Claire and other U.S. cities, they have sought to gather their families, regain self-sufficiency, recover their dignity, and preserve what they can of the culture they have known. No longer Laotian Hmong, they must find a way to live as Hmong Americans.

Hmong children pose next to a livestock fence *in a small village perched high atop the misty mountains of northern Laos, Xieng Khouang Province, 1973.*
Photographer: Wayne Persons.

Chapter I: Across the Mountaintops of Laos

Laos has mountains, the strangest I have ever seen. In some places, thin shafts of limestone stand high, thin and sharp as knife blades. And there are the ones that look like animals, like cats and furry snakes, and like hornless cattle. Much of the mountain country of the north and middle is heavy with brush which on approach turn out to be trees.

Foot trails wind in the canyons by the water courses connecting little villages .... And where the hills are gentle enough so that a man does not fall off, the little fields of slash-and-burn agriculture can be seen from the air ....

"A Letter from John Steinbeck"
Laos, April 1967
(Schanche, vii)

An estimated 7 million Hmong people live in the world today, the vast majority in China's southern provinces. Hmong Americans trace their Chinese ancestry back thousands of years, yet their recent history is rooted in Laos. In the mid-1800s, kinship bonds enabled Hmong families to endure a perilous escape from China. They trekked across rugged mountains to Laos, where they settled around a vast plateau called the Plain of Jars. There, the newcomers grew crops, raised livestock, and bartered for the few goods they could not obtain from the land. Their isolated villages, difficult to reach, offered Hmong limited autonomy, and insulated them from foreign technologies and ideologies.

Approximately 60 ethnic groups inhabited the lands of Laos. The Hmong population grew quickly, yet increased numbers yielded them little leverage with other Laotian peoples. The largest ethnic group, the lowland Lao or Lao Lum, held a disproportionate amount of power. Racial animosity characterized relations between the two. Hmong animism ran at odds with Lao Buddhism. Hmong slash-and-burn agriculture ran counter to Lao paddy cultivation.

When the French invaded Southeast Asia at the end of the 19th century, Hmong leaders sought their patronage. By cultivating relationships with French colonial officials, Hmong leaders climbed the political hierarchy and gained influence. The marriage was an uneasy one, however, causing a rift within Hmong society. World War II radically altered the landscape, widening that rift. Nationalist forces in French Indochina rose up and defeated their colonial rulers in 1954. The governance of Laos remained unsettled as various factions competed for control. Hmong loyalties split apart. Those who had sided with the defeated French found themselves in need of a new foreign patron.

A long time ago, our ancestors Jei Wah Xiong and Nhia Lee Xiong came from ... China. They crossed the Yellow River and then Hu Nan city .... When they got to the border of Laos, which led to the Freezing Death Mountains, my ancestor Nhia Lee told Jei Wah ... "I will not go with you. I will return to China." .... Jei Wah said, "... If you go back, life will not be better. You are my older brother, if you don't want to go, I will go on with our relatives ...." Nhia Lee responded, "You go and find a place to settle, then come back to pick me up. Myself, I choose to stay to see if our cousins come, so we can all live together."

Chia Koua Xiong
Eau Claire, November 5, 1992
Interviewer: Smidchei Xiong
Translator: Pao Lee

Family of Yang Fong Tsang *in Tseo Jia Geo, south of Suifu, Szechuan, China, September 1, 1929. Persecution by Chinese emperors scattered Hmong families, some migrating into Southeast Asia and others remaining in China. Photographer: David C. Graham, National Anthropological Archives, Smithsonian Institution.*

Seeds from China

By correlating archeological and anthropological evidence, oral tradition, and Chinese imperial records, scholars have traced the Hmong to central Asia, possibly as early as 5000 B.C. Hmong folktales describe a place having six months of light and six of dark, where snow lay on mountains and ice covered lakes. Over many centuries, they migrated eastward descending through northeast Tibet into southern China. There, the Chinese referred to them as *Miao* (*Meo* in Southeast Asia), sometimes translated as "barbarians," but actually a variation on the word "man."[1] Their name for themselves — *Hmong* — means "people" although recently, possibly for political reasons, it has been translated as "free people."

For many years the Hmong existed on the fringes of the Chinese empire, on lands less in demand by the ruling population. During the early dynasties, emperors governed frontier minorities by allowing a certain amount of local autonomy, granting noble titles—*kaitong*—to local leaders in exchange for regular tribute and loyalty. This policy was summarized by the phrase: "Cherish the feudal princes, win the distant peoples by kindness and restraint." By granting numerous titles, the Chinese sought to create "a host of squabbling tribal principalities," weakening the Hmong.[2]

The ruling Manchus abandoned this policy in the 17th century, and sought direct control over the lands in Szechwan, Yunnan, Hunan, and Kweichow provinces where the Hmong had established autonomous kingdoms. Military conquest replaced the former policy of "kindness and restraint." Armed pacification campaigns preceded Han-Chinese settlers. Imperial scholars tried to justify land seizures by claiming that the Hmong were misusing the land's resources and, in their "savage and barbaric" state, could only benefit from direct Chinese control.[3]

The Hmong did not submit willingly. Particularly vicious campaigns in 1698, 1732, 1794 and 1855 scattered Hmong families. In the early 1800s, thousands fled southern China and migrated southward into the various kingdoms of Vietnam, Laos and Thailand. Village leaders sent scouts ahead to find suitable lands to farm. Hmong stories refer to these pioneers as seeds, planted in new fields to see if they would grow.[4]

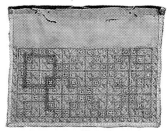

Chinese-style jacket collars, decorated with reverse appliqué, were detached and passed on for generations. Science Museum of Minnesota.

Members of the Lo, Ly, and Moua clans led the migration into northeastern Laos. To avoid confrontation with peoples already inhabiting the lowlands, they settled in the highlands of Xieng Khouang Province around a vast plateau called the Plain of Jars. From there, they gradually spread westward to Luang Prabang, Nam Tha, and Sayaboury. In return for regular tribute paid to the Phouan princes who governed the region, Hmong *kaitong* were left to lead their respective villages. A 1937 population study in French Indochina found nearly 100,000 Hmong living in Vietnam and Laos.[5]

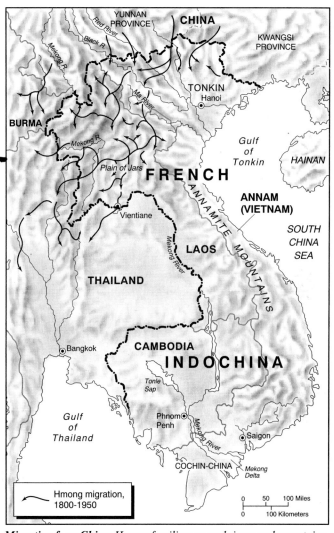

Migrating from China, Hmong families crossed rivers and mountains, concentrating in northern Laos and Vietnam. Map by Carto-Graphics.

I remember going with my parents to the rice field. I remember seeing my parents cut down trees.... They knew how to make axes, long curved knives, smoothing planes, and hoes .... They chopped down trees ... so they could grow rice. They built their houses by hand .... Each year we harvested about 700-800 bushels of rice .... enough for us to eat for a whole year.

Chia Koua Xiong
Eau Claire, November 5, 1992
Interviewer: Smidchei Xiong
Translator: Pao Lee

Hmong farming practices required many hands. *At birth, children received simple necklaces to protect their souls from unfriendly spirits, White Hmong village at Chiang Mai, northern Thailand, ca. 1962-65. Photographer: Surapong Bunnag, National Anthropological Archives, Smithsonian Institution.*

Family Farms

Scattered high atop the rugged Laotian mountains in a multitude of small self-sufficient villages, Hmong people bound themselves to one another through their devotion to family. The household, the most important social unit, frequently included three generations. The householder's authority extended over his wives and children, and their wives and children, whether or not they lived under the same roof.[6] A patrilineal kinship system provided a vital source of social cohesion and political unity. Linguist G. Linwood Barney identified

20 major *xeng,* or clans, in Laos in the 1950s. At birth, a child became a member of the clan of his or her father. As extended family members, clan relatives, no matter how distant, were always welcomed to the home. Cousins referred to one another as brother and sister, and young people deferred to elders. Tradition prohibited members of the same clan from marrying. Parents and local clan leaders sometimes arranged marriages to strengthen political alliances between families.[7] Clan membership played an essential role in wartime. When armed attacks muddied the political situation or scattered villages, individuals depended on family ties.

Average villages ranged in size from 10 to 20 families. Hmong farming methods required many hands, so families tended to be large. The most capable man from the largest clan in a village usually served as its leader, or *naiban.* When necessary, he acted as judge in settling disputes. He took responsibility for overseeing trail maintenance, hosted outside visitors, and organized defense in times of conflict. A *naiban's* authority remained limited, however, as most decisions were arrived at through consensus.[8]

Women possessed little political power. A bride joined the clan and household of her husband, while retaining her maiden name. Women generally did not attend public meetings to resolve village problems, nor did they engage directly in trade. Children were raised with their future roles in mind. At birth, every infant received a simple necklace or bracelet to keep the soul from leaving its body, and to warn spirits that the child was not a slave, but belonged to a family.[9]

Hmong farmers practiced "slash-and-burn" agriculture. During the dry season, men chopped down trees in a forested area. They hauled away larger sections of timber to be used for building materials or firewood. Smaller branches remained to dry in the hot sun providing fuel for dramatic fires. Such fires cleared fields (*daim teb*) designated for planting, and left behind valuable ash to

Above: **Hmong farmers set dramatic fires** *to clear new fields, July 1970. Photographer: Leslie W. Bays, Air America pilot. McDermott Library, University of Texas - Dallas. Below:* **Women plant rice** *in holes punched by men with bamboo poles, northern Laos, May-July 1973. Photographer: W.E. Garrett, ©National Geographic Society. Bottom left to right:* **Taus** *(axe) for tree cutting and splitting firewood and shingles, heavy-headed* **hlau** *(hoe) for breaking rocky soil,* **liag** *(sickle) for harvesting rice. Science Museum of Minnesota.*

15

Mother and children harvest rice outside their village at Nam Tam, northern Laos, May-July 1973. Photographer: W.E. Garrett, ©*National Geographic Society.*

We worked seven days a week.... When the chicken calls, you have to get up and go to the farm .... We had ... acres for rice ... corn ... [and] opium. That's lots of work .... Everything done by hand .... When I was seven or eight ... I was a babysitter, I cut wood, I helped. I care and feed the animals. I went with my father to the farm. I go hunting with my father.

Touly Xiong
Eau Claire, August 12, 1992
Interviewer: Tim Pfaff

fertilize the soil. When Hmong arrived in Indochina, corn represented their main crop because it grew well in the drier highlands. However, through contacts with the midland Khmu and lowland Lao, Hmong farmers began growing highland rice. By the 1940s it had become their staple food source. Farmers continued to grow corn to feed chickens, pigs, and cattle. Those who grew corn only for human consumption were considered lazy or poor. Within the fields, women also tended gardens of cucumbers, melons, yams, eggplant, onions, beans, sugar cane, and various herbs and spices. Fruits such as papayas, bananas, and pineapples also grew well in the lush countryside.[10]

Hmong farming methods were labor intensive. After clearing the fields, every member of the family hurried to plant crops before summer rains began. Often families from the same village cooperated. Village blacksmiths forged tools for the task, and men made use of abundant rattan and bamboo to fashion bins

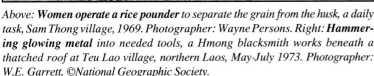

*Above: **Women operate a rice pounder** to separate the grain from the husk, a daily task, Sam Thong village, 1969. Photographer: Wayne Persons. Right: **Hammering glowing metal** into needed tools, a Hmong blacksmith works beneath a thatched roof at Teu Lao village, northern Laos, May-July 1973. Photographer: W.E. Garrett, ©National Geographic Society.*

and baskets for hauling, storing and processing the crops. In this way, villages remained self-sufficient. If a crop failed, villagers pooled their resources so that no family would starve.

After the rains, the Hmong planted poppy seeds for opium, their cash crop. Carrying babies on their backs, mothers weeded fields. Older children minded younger ones, and hauled water to the fields or firewood to the village. At summer's end, families reaped "early rice." In fall, they harvested corn, "late rice," and opium. Rice had to be gathered quickly before too much was lost to the birds or the wind. With their crops in storage bins, Hmong families celebrated the festival of the New Year and prepared for the agricultural cycle to begin again.

After a few years in the same location, nearby fields became exhausted, so farmers had to travel further from their villages each day to work. Sometimes men built small shelters to stay in while tilling distant fields. When even this became impractical, farmers sought out new lands and households or entire villages relocated. For this reason, farmers did not build large, permanent houses. Strong, lightweight bamboo, tied with hemp, formed the framework for a peaked-roof shelter. Using axes, hammers, and wedges, men splintered large and small shingles from hardwood trunks to fill in the walls or roof. Thatched elephant grass also served for roofing material.

17

Inside, Hmong houses usually consisted of one large multi-purpose room and one or two smaller rooms for sleeping. Women cooked soups and rice over large earthen stoves. Over a small fire on the dirt floor, a metal tripod held a wok for quick frying meats and vegetables.[11] Since rice was eaten at every meal, pounding rice to separate the grain from the husk was a daily chore. Children sometimes wore a carrying basket laden with rocks to give themselves enough weight to push down the heavy rice pounder. Metal cooking pans, one large for pig mash and the other smaller for family meals, could be bartered from traveling merchants. Men hollowed stumps to fashion wooden rice cookers.

Hunting for Food

Back then [1940s], Hmong used crossbows to kill squirrels and birds. They were able to kill some, but it was insufficient. I told my father, "I would like to buy a Hmong hand-made gun." It cost four silver bars which was equivalent to $800. My brother and I each bought a gun. We went deer hunting, wild pig hunting, and bear hunting in the jungle. In Laos, a hunting license was not required ....When I wasn't working and there weren't any visitors around, I took my relatives and we went deer hunting. I had a good hunting dog .... it would chase deer .... I bought this dog for one silver bar .... Each time we went hunting, we killed one or two deer. If we had ten people, I would divide the meat into ten piles.

Chia Koua Xiong
Eau Claire, November 5, 1992
Interviewer: Smidchei Xiong
Translator: Pao Lee

In Laos, "hunting season" lasted year-round. Farmers carried hand-made crossbows or muskets to the fields in the morning. On their way, they set snares or traps to catch wild roosters or grouse. A common snare, the *hlua ncaws* ("hlooa njer"), was used to catch birds. A hunter looped a cord at the opening of a bamboo tube, and then baited it with a worm or piece of corn. When the bird reached its head in to eat, the snare tripped and caught the bird. After working in the fields, farmers hunted for a few hours or emptied traps on the way home.[12]

From a young age, boys learned to trap squirrels and rats, or catch birds on bamboo perches smeared with tree sap. As men, they hunted deer, wild boars, bears, and even tigers, sometimes luring prey with a tamed rooster.[13] Wild boar could be especially dangerous because they charged when cornered. If a hunter's gun misfired, he might be sliced open by a boar's sharp tusks.

Above: **Hunting with a locally forged flintlock,** *Paksong, Xieng Khouang Province, 1966. Photographer: Wayne Persons. Below:* **Tawb nas qaib** *(rooster carry cage), for carrying live bait to lure game. Science Museum of Minnesota.*

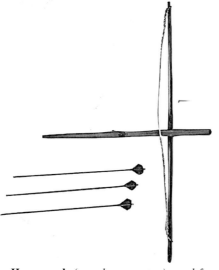

Hneev, xub *(crossbow, arrows), used for small game, arrows were sometimes tipped with locally made poisons. Science Museum of Minnesota.*

Hmong women gather in the light of the doorway to do their needlework, Mykply village, Sayaboury Province, 1968. Photographer: Terry Wofford.

Creating "Flower Cloth"

Besides weeding fields, cooking meals, and caring for children, Hmong women also made clothing for their families. In Laos, clothing styles provided one indication of Hmong subgroups. For example, Blue/Green Hmong women wore elaborately decorated skirts which contrasted with the plain white pleated skirts of White Hmong. Striped Hmong women wore tops with alternating dark blue and black stripes encircling the sleeves. This visual division perhaps dates back to Hmong origins in China. Oral tradition relates that a Chinese emperor hoped to divide and weaken the Hmong by arbitrarily ordering certain villages to dress differently.[14] After generations in Laos, ceremonies and dialetical variatons in language further distinguished the numerous subgroups.

Before they could buy cloth from traveling merchants, women cultivated and processed hemp (*maj*) for cloth. The wearisome process required months of planting and weeding fields, harvesting and hand-

*Above: **Fold and tuck work** by Xao Y. Lee, in progress, Sheboygan (WI), 1985. Below: **Rooster style hat** in elaborate appliqué and fold and tuck work, decorated with pom-pons. Elizabeth Perkins Collection.*

19

Winding hemp in northern Thailand, 1967. National Anthropological Archives, Smithsonian Institution.

I learn about eight years old. My mom teach me to do Hmong custom dress ... to do cross-stitch ... the [Blue Hmong] skirt .... I start on the bottom part cross-stitch and my mom do the batik on the top, ... and after she done with the dye and everything, I help her to put appliqué on top and bottom .... Usually Hmong girls learn about cross-stitch when they're young .... When they are walking to the field, they just carry it ... and keep walking and sewing ... If you have a lot of time and didn't do anything [else] ... maybe four or five months, but in Laos ... you can do only one per year.

Tang Kue
Menomonie (WI), March 8, 1993
Interviewer: Tim Pfaff

Blue/Green Hmong skirt, *batiked, finger-pleated and decorated with cross-stitch and ribbon appliqué, made by Mai Xao Yang. Hmong speakers use the same word for "blue" and "green." Elizabeth Perkins Collection.*

stripping stalks, and spinning, bleaching and weaving fibers. Despite the amount of work required, hemp skirts were favored particularly among White Hmong women because of the hemp's durability and ability to hold pleats.[15] In the 20th century, cotton became a ready substitute as better roads to villages encouraged trade. Imported French trade cloth, beads, and silver coins also began to appear as decorative additions.

Hmong girls learned to sew at a young age and took years to master numerous techniques which they referred to as *paj ntaub* ("pandao"), or flower cloth. They made the most of natural light, carrying needlework to fields or sewing in the doorways of their homes. Skillfully decorated clothing reflected a family's wealth and factored into a young girl's marriage prospects. Needleworkers colored cloth with native vegetable dyes and added appliqued or cross-stitched designs which were passed down by generations of women. In the 19th century, the Hmong were not known to have a written language. However, folk stories relate that they once used a written script which was banned by a Chinese emperor. Hmong women were said to have incorporated the characters into their needlework in an attempt to preserve the script.

While colorful, some clothing also functioned to ward off or fool unfriendly spirits. A shaman might prescribe a cross to be added to a patient's shirt for protection.

A mother shops in a *Sayaboury market. Batiked and appliqued designs on the baby-carrier are intended to guard her child from unfriendly spirits, 1968. Photographer: Terry Wofford.*

Mothers wrapped infants in vivid baby-carriers and dressed them in tassled, multi-colored hats. The children were thus disguised as flowers in hopes of protecting them from unfriendly spirits who might attempt to lure away their souls.[16]

Shaman - Soul Caller

Hmong spiritual beliefs combined ancestor veneration, commonly practiced in China, with animism. Spirits called *dab* ("da") inhabited all things in the Hmong world. Throughout their lives, Hmong people offered animal sacrifices and performed ritual ceremonies to maintain good relations with the *dab* of the home, field, and forest. Appropriate ceremonies in the fields were as important to a bountiful crop as adequate rain or rich soil. In addition, not all *dab* were friendly, so it was especially important to enlist the aid of helper spirits through regular offerings.[17] The *txiv neeb* ("tsee neng"), or shaman, acted as spiritual guide and healer, erecting altars in homes, and placing shrines in fields and along trails. Shamans, male or female, often received their calling as a result of enduring a serious illness during which they had been rendered unconscious. They were chosen and given special powers by helper *dab* through dreams.

By reading signs and communicating with the spirits, the shaman determined whether a spiritual or physical problem had caused illness. If the cause was physical, an herbalist, usually a woman, prepared a remedy. The shaman battled spiritual illnesses which occurred when souls had been frightened or lured away from their bodies by unfriendly *dab*. The sick person was laid next to an altar equipped with offerings of incense, rice, and wine, and protected by swords and brass bells. The shaman placed a veil over his or her head, entered a deep trance and began involuntarily shaking. An assistant beat a sacred gong to frighten unfriendly *dab*. Spirit helpers accompanied the shaman who searched for the lost soul. At the end of the ceremony, lasting many hours, the shaman tossed the split horn of a buffalo on the ground, reading the pieces to decide upon an appropriate sacrifice.[18]

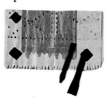

Ntawv txam *(spirit money)*, **ntxheej txam** *(spirit money tool)*, *design by Neng Lor Lee. Spirit money lines a shaman's altar, and may be offered to spirits in exchange for their help.*

*A **shaman spoons rice and wine offerings** for spirits at a baby-naming ceremony, Teu La, northern Laos, May-July 1973. Photographer: W.E. Garrett, ©National Geographic Society.*

Those two [helper spirits], Leng Nko and Cheng Xeng, they are the ones that tell you why the person is sick, what is wrong with his/her spirit, why the spirit is not staying with the person's body. They also tell you where the person's spirit has fallen - to which cemetery or hole - so that you will know what kind of animal to sacrifice .... the animal spirit will live in there, and if the devil spirit comes close to the person's spirit, then the animal's spirit will bite or fight with the devil spirit.

Neng Lor Lee
Eau Claire, December 18, 1992
Interviewer: James P. Leary
Translator: Kao Xiong

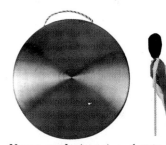

Nruas neeb *(gong) and* **qws ruas** *(beater), made by Sia Vang Xiong. Science Museum of Minnesota. An assistant beats the gong while the shaman visits the spirit world to ward off unfriendly spirits and invite helper spirits.*

Tais qe hu nplig *(eggs for spiritual renewal), one egg for each member of the family with incense burned to invite helper spirits. The eggs represent the life cycle and, after a special New Year ceremony, are eaten by family members.*

Ball tossing during New Year celebration, *a courting game, White Hmong village at Chiang Mai, northern Thailand, ca. 1962-65. Photographer: Surapong Bunnag, National Anthropological Archives, Smithsonian Institution.*

New Year: Celebrating the Harvest

Xim xaus *(violin), played for courtship, weddings and at New Year, made by Kao Xiong.*

With the full moon in the twelfth month of the year, the Hmong celebrated New Year, the harvest festival. Families and relatives from distant villages came together for three entertaining days of eating, games, music, and courting. It was a time to honor all living things. Houses were ritually swept clean of the past year, and incense was burned to invite in the new. Elders and village leaders led special ceremonies, expressing their gratitude for the past year's bounty while casting aside its misfortunes. Sacrifices of pigs or chickens appeased the spirits of forests and fields and honored house spirits, ancestors and the souls of living family members.

Qeej musician dances at New Year at Sam Thong, 1969. Photographer: Wayne Persons.

Xauv nyiaj *(necklace), White Hmong, made from four* choj *(bars) of silver by Pa Chou Vang who apprenticed under his brother-in-law, Ga Chue Yang, at Pha Khao, Xieng Khouang Province, in the early 1960s. Eau Claire Area Hmong Mutual Assistance Association.*

Throughout the year, Hmong women, young and old, worked on elaborately embroidered costumes for themselves and their families. At New Year they adorned clothing with heavy silver necklaces, an indication of a family's wealth and, in an economy without cash, a useful method of transporting family assets. Young girls wore their new costumes to courting games, tossing cloth balls to suitors who wooed them with love songs. Married men gambled on fighting bulls and horse races. Musicians filled the air with sounds of Hmong violins and flutes. *Qeej* players competed in musical contests, performing difficult acrobatic dance maneuvers.

During New Year's time - no work, but eat and ball tossing and do a lot of folk singing .... My first time, most embarrassing in my life .... I was first time to get over to the ball field with my older friends ... They asked me to go ... to toss ball back and forth .... The older sisters, they found the lovers or boys to toss [with], because boys come and ask .... An uncle of mine look for whole morning and he had not found anybody .... Then finally he came to me and ask me to toss - he was looking good - so I say sure. I toss with him for a couple minutes, then finally one of my cousins know ... that we are related, we are the same name [clan] ... He pull my uncle away from me and another cousin come and say "Oh, shame on you! You do not toss with your own name, Vue." So I say "Well, I did not know he is a Vue."

Houa Vue Moua
Eau Claire, May 10, 1993
Interviewer: Tim Pfaff

Wearing her family's wealth, *a young women poses in her New Year's outfit with heavy silver necklaces and French coins, Teu La, May - July, 1973. Photographer: W.E. Garrett, ©National Geographic Society.*

Harvesting poppies in Phou Chai, Luang Prabang Province, ca. 1960s. Photographer: Wayne Persons. The woman is Yao, denoted by the red fringe around her neck. Hmong, Yao, and other highlanders raised opium as a cash crop.

Poppies for the French: Cash, Taxes and Power

For several generations, Hmong villagers lived in remote northern Laos far from the gaze of British and French colonialists. By the mid-19th century, however, the European powers had focused their sights and military might eastward. The lands and peoples of Asia became prizes in a great political and economic rivalry. Hmong cultivation of opium for barter eventually drew the attention of powerful colonial interests, producing an alliance with far-reaching political consequences.

In the 1850s, France looked with envy at British control of the lucrative "China trade." British steamers, docking at Shanghai and Canton, enjoyed exclusive access to China's seemingly limitless markets and reaped huge profits for investors in England. Unable to challenge the British openly, the French sought indirect access through Indochina. By navigating the Mekong and Red rivers, they hoped to bypass the China coast and forge their own alliances in the interior. Naval expeditions were dispatched beginning in 1858. By 1861, the French had established a garrison at Saigon, facilitating annexation of Cochin China (Saigon and the Mekong Delta). In the following decades, the French used military might and diplomatic subterfuge to conquer local opposition. By 1893 they had overcome armed resistance in Vietnam, Laos, and Cambodia and established French Indochina.[19]

Dreaming of rich profits, the French divided Indochina into political spheres convenient to their economic interests. Surveyors set the borders of Laos to coincide with the Mekong watershed ignoring existing political structures and the distribution of Laos' multi-ethnic society. Groups such as the Hmong found they had relatives on opposite borders, sometimes governed by antagonistic groups. The new lines also inhibited the Hmong and other highlanders who moved often in search of fertile lands.[20]

With the 1893 annexation of Laos, Parisian investors shipped 15 tons of trade goods to posts on the Mekong. The river was poorly suited for transportation however, and the venture quickly collapsed. The French, forced to cut expenses, minimized their colonial staff and created a hierarchy that granted considerable local autonomy. They administered the remote northern highlands through the existing network of leaders. Six to ten villages, each governed by local *naiban*, formed a *tasseng* or sub-district directed by an elected Hmong official (also called *tasseng)*. Approximately 10 *tasseng* formed a *muong,* or district, supervised by a *chaomuong.* Although the lowland Lao made up only 45 percent of the population, they and a large number of educated Vietnamese dominated colonial government. King Sisavang Vong and the Lao royal family remained at Luang Prabang, the traditional capital, a symbolic gesture to bolster popular support. Hmong and other minorities had little voice at the political capital, Vientiane.[21]

To make French Indochina profitable, Governor-General Paul Doumer directed his attention away from China to the growing opium trade. Since annexing Saigon in 1862, the French had taxed the trade to pay for the development of infrastructure. In 1899, Doumer moved further by establishing an official government opium monopoly. He built a refinery in Saigon, processing imported opium to be sold throughout Indochina. Within a few years, revenues increased by 50 percent and the colonial treasury for the first time showed a surplus. From 1899-1939, the monopoly imported 60 tons of raw opium each year from Iran and Turkey. The government licensed 2,500 dens and retail shops in Indochina in 1939, supplying more than 100,000 addicts. Tax revenues from the trade solidified the colonial treasury and, by attracting other investors, indirectly financed colonial railways, schools and hospitals.[22]

In 1939, World War II erupted in Europe. Japan occupied Indochina the following year, but temporarily left French administrators in their positions. Cut off from Mid-East suppliers, the French turned to Hmong farmers whose opium was highly regarded.[23] Opium poppies required soil and weather conditions found at altitudes above 3,000 feet. In Xieng Khouang and Sam Neua provinces, raw opium was worth its weight in silver. Hmong farmers valued the easily transported

Weighing raw opium in Xieng Khouang Province, ca. 1954. Alfred W. McCoy. In 1971, traders paid highland farmers $500 for 10 kilos of opium. Converted to heroin, it would sell for $225,000 on the streets of New York.

crop and traded most of it to Chinese and Lao merchants for silver, salt, cloth, and tools. Small amounts were used for medicinal purposes to combat diarrhea, and by older people as a pain reliever for aching joints. A strong village work ethic discouraged addiction.[24]

Twenty years before, the French had tried to increase the local supply of opium. Their demand had been made clumsily, through local Thai and Lao administrators without consulting Hmong leaders who viewed it as the latest in a string of discriminatory actions. As a result, a bloody rebellion swept across northern Vietnam and Laos from 1919 to 1921. Rebel leader Pa Chai Vue called for an independent Hmong kingdom centered at Dien Bien Phu in northwest Vietnam.[25] The rebellion created a colonial crisis and was quelled only after regular troops were mobilized from Saigon and Hanoi. After that experience, the French dealt more carefully with the Hmong, not wanting to risk a second rebellion in such a remote section of Indochina.

Nyiaj choj *(silver bars), one* choj *(380 grams) of opium was worth one silver bar (380 grams). Parents horded silver to buy trade goods, fashion jewelry, or help their sons pay a bride price.*

In 1940, rather than using Lao intermediaries, the French worked through Touby Lyfoung, recently elected *tasseng* at Nong Het in Xieng Khouang Province. Lyfoung was a member of the prominent Ly clan and one of a few Hmong to be educated in the French colonial school system. A year earlier, he had begun an eight-year tenure as the only Hmong member of the Opium Purchasing Board. Lyfoung raised the annual head tax in the Nong Het district from three silver piasters to eight. Knowing that most Hmong farmers would be either unable or unwilling to part with such a large amount of silver, he gave them the option of paying instead in opium. The new tax produced an opium boom in Nong Het and was soon applied throughout the region. In just a few years, Indochina's opium production increased by 800 percent, rising to 60.6 tons in 1944. Colonial officer Charles Rochet remarked a few years later: "Opium used to be one of the nobles of the land; today it is king."[26]

Touby Lyfoung speaking with French officer on the Plain of Jars, 1953. Alfred W. McCoy.

Before World War II, the French Government bought opium in Afghanistan and India, and warehoused it at Hanoi. During the war, when they could no longer import it, they encouraged local poppy-growing so that the Chinese, the Vietnamese, and French smokers in the colony could still get their supplies .... The crop was grown mainly by Meo [Hmong] tribes, and the Yaos, and to some extent by the Lahus and Lissus [sic] ...Opium from Xieng Khouang and Sam Neua was especially prized. It only had a seven percent morphine content but according to those who smoked it, the flavor was excellent.

... In each province, the French set up buying offices where the opium was bought. But first they tried to deal directly with the producers, which didn't work out. They couldn't pay the producers until they knew the morphine content of their opium, and analyses took several weeks. The unfortunate growers were so poor, they couldn't wait that long. So the French had to use middlemen, usually Chinese merchants who had some capital and were able to advance money. There were also Vietnamese, Lao, and a few Meo [Hmong] who had grown rich. These "brokers" paid for the crop in cash, making sure that there was a handsome margin between the price they paid the peasants, and the price they received from the French Authorities. They paid the growers in silver bullion from the Bank of Indochina, or else with goods of various kinds costed on the full price. So they made a double profit.

Touby Lyfoung, 1972
(Lamour, 116-17)

Touby Lyfoung's success endeared him to the French. The relationship was further enhanced by his ability to organize Hmong militia to resist the Japanese occupation. In 1944 a team of Free French commandos led by Second Lieutenant Maurice Gauthier, clandestinely parachuted into northern Laos along with thousands of pounds of ammunition and explosives. Since French intelligence officers would be easily spotted by the Japanese, Gauthier's team quickly linked up with the Hmong militia. Accustomed to the rugged terrain, Hmong guerrillas traversed mountain trails quickly without attracting undue attention. For the remainder of the occupation, Hmong villagers harbored French soldiers while guerrillas gathered intelligence and harrassed Japanese patrols.[27]

After Japan's defeat, the communist Vietminh (Vietnam Independence League) and Lao Issara (Free Lao) led growing nationalist movements that tried to prevent the return of the French colonialists. The French rewarded Touby Lyfoung's continued assistance by appointing him *chaomuong* (district administrator), for the first time granting the Hmong direct representation at the national level.[28] The Hmong, however, were not united behind the French. By supporting Touby Lyfoung, the French had betrayed his political rival, Lo Faydang Bliayao, and inflamed a long-standing feud between the Lo and Ly clans. In 1935, the French had promised the Nong Het position to Lo Faydang, but four years later they did not deem him sufficiently loyal and barred him from the election.

Lo Faydang grew embittered against colonial rule. He recruited farmers driven into debt by Touby Lyfoung's heavy "opium tax," a hardship which sometimes compelled families to sell their children. After World War II, his Hmong Resistance League joined the Vietnamese and Lao resistance to France's return to power.[29] The rivalry between the two men became a lasting one with significant consequences for the Laotian Hmong during the next chapter of Southeast Asia's history.

The Hmong could walk eight to ten miles an hour for 48 hours. I considered myself in top physical shape, but in the early days I had great difficulty in keeping the Hmong pace. In the jungle, I struggled to follow the pace of the man before me. I was amazed that the Hmong approached a mountaintop by heading straight for its peak. None of this winding up the mountain. One day, I asked the men with me why they always walked straight to the top of a mountain. All of them looked at me in disbelief. One man answered simply: "That's where we're going."

French 2nd Lt. Maurice Gauthier
Jane Hamilton-Merritt (31)

American and Thai instructors train Hmong recruits at Pha Khao, Xieng Khouang Province, ca. 1961-63. Lloyd "Pat" Landry Papers, History of Aviation Collection, McDermott Library, University of Texas - Dallas. Landry was among the first CIA case officers sent into northern Laos in 1961.

Chapter II: The Secret War

French control of Indochina collapsed in 1954 at Dien Bien Phu. The Vietnamese celebrated the liberation of their country as the end of "colonialism." Americans labelled it "communist aggression." Anti-communism had become the litmus test for American politicians. Successive U.S. Presidents pursued the policy of "containment," arguing that communism had to be fought on every front, or one by one, like dominos, nations around the world would fall. U.S. interests in Asia appeared vulnerable. American prestige had been stung by the "loss" of China and an unsatisfactory stalemate in Korea. Southeast Asia became a symbolic but bloody battleground, swept up in the ideological clash between the capitalist United States and the communist Soviet Union.

President Eisenhower refused to deploy troops, but committed advisors and materiel to strengthen anti-communist leaders in Vietnam, Laos and Cambodia. In Laos, American dollars financed public works projects, funded a 25,000 man Royal Laotian Army, and helped fix elections for pro-western candidates. However, by prohibiting the communist Pathet Lao and its political wing, the *Neo Lao Hak Sat* (NLHS - Lao Patriotic Front), from legitimate participation in the country's governance, the Americans unwittingly pushed them toward armed resistance. The Pathet Lao allied itself with the North Vietnamese, and found its own powerful patrons in the Soviet Union and China.

In 1961 President Kennedy chose to make a stand in Vietnam rather than Laos. Vietnam's extensive coastline presented strategic advantages for the direct application of U.S. air and sea power. Laos, however, lined Vietnam's western border, and so could not be overlooked. Along a network of trails known collectively as the Ho Chi Minh Trail, the North Vietnamese and their Laotian allies funneled supplies through Laos to South Vietnam. To cut off those supplies, Kennedy ordered operatives from the U.S. Central Intelligence Agency (CIA) to recruit a secret army of Laotian and Vietnamese highlanders.

Hmong loyalties were split. Lo Faydang Bliayao and his Hmong Resistance League joined the Pathet Lao. Touby Lyfoung and emerging military leader Vang Pao negotiated an alliance with the Americans. Others simply tried to steer clear of the fighting. By 1964 General Vang Pao commanded nearly 30,000 men. Hmong soldiers ambushed communist supply lines, guarded radar installations which guided U.S. bombers over North Vietnam, and acted as the front-line defense of Laos. Supplied entirely by the United States, the army remained secret to avoid the appearance of violating the 1962 Geneva Accords which prohibited foreign intervention in Laos. Later, with American soldiers fighting and dying in Vietnam, U.S. leaders feared the public's reaction to a widening war in faraway Southeast Asia.

The Neo Lao Hak Sat (Lao Patriotic Front) prints newspapers and propaganda leaflets *inside one of many caves in northern Laos, January 1966. AP/Wide World Photos. The Pathet Lao operation claimed to have more than 50 staff people.*

Nationalism in Indochina

Japan's surrender in 1945 officially ended the carnage of World War II, but it by no means resolved the political situation in Southeast Asia. Neither Vietnam nor Laos could escape the long shadow of events unfolding in post-war Europe. The Soviet Union, an ally of the United States during the war, now emerged as its most powerful enemy. The Soviet Red Army occupied Eastern Europe and showed little inclination to withdraw. France, Italy, and other European countries had been severely weakened by the war and now faced the staggering task of reconstruction. Their governments remained unstable as rival factions, among them communists, competed for political influence. The United States placed a high priority on France's recovery and reluctantly agreed to support its wish to resume control of Indochina.

The war had lingering effects in Indochina as well. Vietminh nationalists had gained strength and confidence resisting the Japanese occupation. By the summer of 1945, they had organized a provisional government, and on September 2nd announced the formation of the Democratic Republic of Vietnam (DRV). The Allies mistrusted popular DRV leader Ho Chi Minh because of his communist ties. They refused Vietnamese pleas to recognize their new government, and proceeded with plans to return the French to power. In southern Vietnam below the 16th parallel, British forces were assigned to receive the Japanese surrender, and immediately stepped aside for the French. In northern Vietnam, the situation was complicated by the strength of the Vietminh and the presence of Chinese Nationalist troops. As a political concession, the French recognized the DRV within a French Union and sent troops to replace the Chinese. In November 1946, a dispute over the administration of Haiphong Harbor led to a French attack on the city. The Vietnam War had begun.[30]

Senator Joseph McCarthy's outspoken attacks against "anti-American" *activities fed widespread paranoia about communism which encouraged U.S. involvement in Southeast Asia, June 9, 1954. State Historical Society of Wisconsin. WHi (x3) 19890.*

Emulating the tactics of Mao Tse-tung's "people's war," Ho Chi Minh's forces prepared for an all-out struggle to "liberate" Vietnam. They campaigned throughout the countryside to win the hearts and minds of the people. From hidden bases in the mountains along the Laos-Vietnam border, they recruited village farmers and intimidated dissenters. The French relied heavily on fortified garrisons in the cities, pursuing a more traditional strategy which emphasized the winning and holding of territory. They also tried to exploit long-standing ethnic divisions and reduce the Vietminh's pool of support by recruiting minority highlanders to gather intelligence and disrupt supply lines.

Despite early French advances, the North Vietnamese Army (PAVN) grew stronger with each passing year. The 1949 communist victory in China intensified the conflict and, from an American perspective, raised the stakes. Mao Tse Tung's forces funneled Chinese and Soviet supplies to the PAVN. The United States simultaneously increased its already substantial material support of France. U.S. National Security Council Study 48/2 declared on December 30, 1949 that the United States should "scrutinize closely the development of threats from Communist aggression, direct or indirect, and be prepared to help within our means by providing political, economic, and military assistance and advice .... Particular attention should be given to the problem of Indochina."[31]

In Laos, the nationalist movement had also grown during the Japanese occupation. In 1941, Japan forced King Sisavang Vong to cede Laotian territory west of the Mekong to Thailand, its ally. The French

31

perceived the Thai as a growing threat. They sought a way to prevent Pan-Thai propaganda from crossing the Mekong and further weakening their position. Colonial officer Charles Rochet spearheaded a nationalist movement to counter Thai propaganda by promoting Lao literature and music, building schools, creating a national development program, and sponsoring patriotic marches and rallies. The campaign worked too well, arousing long-suppressed Lao nationalist sentiments that the French could not control.[32]

I heard there had been a great battle and that the townspeople had fought very bravely against the French. I thought it would be very good if we could fight against the same enemy. I went down to the plains myself and tried to find this prince [Souphanouvong] .... I sent him a message and the reply came back: "Arouse the people. Create a strong organization. Later we will fight together." So I returned to the mountains and began to organize all the [Hmong] villages from our own base .... Every village appointed organizers and formed scouts and defense corps.

Lo Faydang Bliayao, 1957
Interviewer: Wilfred Burchett
(Dommen, 7)

Training soldiers in Touby Lyfoung's militia *to use a machine gun, ca. 1954. Alfred W. McCoy. Hmong militias aided the French during the Japanese occupation and eased their return to Laos after World War II.*

In 1945 the Japanese implemented a coup and pressured King Sisavang Vong to declare independence from France. After Japan's defeat, the King's son, Prince Phetsarath, tried to maintain that independence by arguing that since the French had been unable to protect Laos during the war, they no longer had authority to resume power. He formed a new government called the *Lao Issara* (Free Laos). The King disagreed. He welcomed the French and stripped Phetsarath of all offices, yet the monarch's support in Vientiane was limited.[33] Members of the ruling Lao elite remained divided over whether to ally themselves with the Vietminh or pursue Laotian independence through the French. Both choices carried the danger of foreign domination.

Phetsarath's brother, Souvanna Phouma, and half-brother, Souphanouvong, emerged to lead competing factions. A neutralist, Souvanna Phouma favored a government of national reconciliation that included all political factions. Souphanouvong distrusted the French and felt that Laotian independence could only be won by force. When the Lao Issara collapsed from infighting, he sought support from the Vietminh. With their help, Souphanouvong organized a resistance government in 1950 called the *Pathet Lao* (Land of the Lao) and was joined by Hmong leader Lo Faydang Bliayao and his Hmong Resistance League.[34]

Like its North Vietnamese counterpart, the Pathet Lao professed a communist doctrine, yet its supporters were first and foremost nationalists. In Laos, unlike many Third World countries where revolutions have occurred, the land and its riches were not owned by a tiny elite. The Pathet Lao could not attract followers by proposing aggressive land reform. They appealed instead to nationalist, anti-colonial sentiments. They spent time with villagers in the countryside promoting a multi-ethnic state, while the Royal Lao Government (RLG) remained isolated in Vientiane and focused only on the lowland Lao.[35] Lo Faydang's support of the Pathet Lao can be traced in part to the earlier French betrayal and his bitter rivalry with Touby Lyfoung.

The Pathet Lao attracted an increasing number of supporters, yet its field organization paled in comparison to that of the North Vietnamese. The People's Army of North Vietnam (PAVN) shuffled supplies and troops along the mountainous trails of Phong Saly and Sam Neua provinces, but clearly their priority remained Vietnam. The French built on their alliance with Touby Lyfoung and continued to recruit Hmong and other Laotian highlanders. Well-adapted to the rugged mountains, Hmong guerrillas applied the same hit-and-run tactics in Laos that the PAVN was employing so successfully in Vietnam.

Northern Laos offered both sides a strategic location and an economic resource which could materially aid their efforts. When the PAVN invaded northern Laos in 1953, one of their objectives was to secure the annual opium crop, needed to buy arms and ammunition. On the black market, six kilograms of opium bought a light machine gun and 500 rounds of ammunition; four kilos purchased an automatic rifle and 500 rounds. The French and Touby Lyfoung's forces fought to protect the crop, which from 1946-54 represented their own source of military funding. Code-named "Operation X," the opium trade (officially banned in 1950) enabled French intelligence officers to recruit, train, and equip Laotian highlanders covertly.[36]

In April 1953, the Vietnamese 316th People's Army Division, Pathet Lao irregulars, and Lo Faydang's Hmong militia captured Xieng Khouang City. From the surrounding hills, Touby Lyfoung's militia kept them hemmed in while the French airlifted troops and artillery onto the nearby Plain of Jars. Together they were able by the year's end to drive the communists out of Xieng Khouang Province. Notably, Civil Air Transport (later renamed Air America), an airline owned and operated by the CIA, flew U.S. Air Force transports with French markings to resupply those forces in northeastern Laos. CIA operative Colonel Edward Landsdale had witnessed Hmong maneuvers during his six week tour of Indochina in the summer of 1953. His observations no doubt influenced President Eisenhower's decision to deploy U.S. Special Forces advisory teams in 1959. The teams recruited and trained Laotian highlanders in guerrilla warfare to support American initiatives in Southeast Asia. Landsdale later remarked: "The main thought was to have an early warning, trip wire sort of thing with these tribes in the mountains getting intelligence on North Vietnamese movements.... saving the rice-producing lowlands of Thailand and Vietnam by sealing off the mountain infiltration routes from China and North Vietnam."[37]

As the war intensified, mounting French casualties weakened support in Paris and cries for a diplomatic settlement grew louder. The turning point came in 1954 at Dien Bien Phu. By garrisoning a large number of troops and supplies in the bowl-shaped valley of northwest Vietnam, General Henri Navarre hoped to lure the PAVN into a more traditional pitched battle where the French would have the advantage. Dien Bien Phu's location would also enable the French garrison to confront future PAVN invasions of Laos.[38] The North Vietnamese defied Navarre by using thousands of soldiers and coolies to haul heavy artillery up the steep mountain slopes. Once in place on peaks surrounding the garrison, their guns pounded French positions. The day before delegates met in Geneva to negotiate a peaceful settlement of the conflict, Dien Bien Phu was overrun.

My initial conversation with Touby was straightforward. I told him the Allies were considering invading the area, more troops would be arriving and we were preparing to fight the Japanese. I asked him what he thought, and he said, "I'm with you." He said he was willing to cooperate and bring his people into the fight together with us. We agreed to give weapons to his people, train them to use them, and lead them into the fight. There was no question of money; there was no question of mercenaries. I think Touby saw in this an opportunity of gaining better positions for his people, politically.

Maurice Gauthier
Interview, July 1988
(Hamilton-Merritt, 27-28)

... Our main task was to convince the world that the Southeast Asia war was an aggressive move by the Communists to subjugate the entire area. To make this clear was a real necessity: our people as well as the citizens of the three Associated States of Indochina [Vietnam, Laos and Cambodia] had to be assured of the true meaning of the war.

Dwight D. Eisenhower
Mandate for Change 1953-56
McCoy & Adams (140)

Air dropping supplies to soldiers and civilians in northern Laos, ca. 1960s. Timothy Castle. American air mobility was essential in Laos due to the rugged terrain and scarcity of roads. Air America pilot Robert Hifler identified four primary flying hazards: tricky winds, monsoons, the "smokey season" [slash-and-burn farming], and, in clear weather, "unfriendly folk who had a good shot at you."

Although not signatory to the 1954 Geneva Accords and thus not legally bound by them, the Americans exerted substantial influence to further their anti-communist agenda. The Accords divided Vietnam nearly in half at the 17th parallel and made provision for elections to be held in July 1956 to reunify the country. (Such elections were never held). They further guaranteed the territorial integrity of Laos and Cambodia and called for free and open elections. Laos was to remain neutral and refrain from entering into military alliances. Foreign countries were prohibited from direct interference in Laotian internal affairs, and foreign military assistance was to be limited to that necessary to enable Laos to maintain its own defense. The Pathet Lao were to regroup in the two northern provinces of Sam Neua and Phong Saly "pending their integration into the Lao army or demobilization."[39]

The Eisenhower Administration sought to contain the North Vietnamese by creating and fortifying viable pro-western governments in South Vietnam, Laos, and Cambodia. Laos was labelled a key "domino." J. Graham Parsons, U.S. Assistant Secretary for Far Eastern Affairs, described Laos as the "finger thrust right into the heart of Southeast Asia."[40] A communist Laos, so the thinking went, would jeopardize South Vietnam, Cambodia, Thailand, and Burma. By the same token, the North Vietnamese also recognized the potential benefits of a Laotian client state, and the corresponding dangers of a foe along its western border. Officially and publicly, Laos remained neutral. In fact, Laos became deeply embroiled in the growing hostilities in Vietnam, exploited by both sides to gain strategic advantage.

The Americans searched in Laos for a strong anti-communist leader or, at least, a neutralist government that did not include the communist Neo Lao Hak Sat (NLHS - Lao Patriotic Front), the political arm of the Pathet Lao. The United States heavily subsidized the Laotian economy, quickly becoming the largest single source of income. In 1955 alone, the Americans funded eleven public works projects at a cost of approximately $1.4 million.[41] The Royal Lao Army (RLA) received the lion's share of U.S. funding, during the 1950s nearly 80 percent of an estimated $40 million.

Such overwhelming dependence offered U.S. policymakers extraordinary leverage with Laotian prime ministers.[42] By withholding monthly payments, the United States could easily cripple the Laotian economy and force a vote of no confidence in an uncooperative government.

Prior to the 1958 spring elections, U.S. Ambassador to Laos J. Graham Parsons devised "Operation Booster Shot," a crash program designed to win victories for pro-Western candidates. The program funded highly visible public works projects such as repairs on schools and Buddhist temples, construction of first-aid stations and dispensaries, and in remote areas, air drops of food and medical supplies. Many pro-Western candidates were also given credit lines which they used to purchase merchandise to buy votes. The $3 million program backfired. Pathet Lao candidates denounced it as a glaring example of government corruption. The Pathet Lao won 9 of 21 contested seats, a stunning defeat for the Americans. The results reflected two profound weaknesses of pro-western Royalist candidates. First, they were perceived as pawns of the Americans, the new colonialists. Second, they remained out of touch with the rural population and antagonistic to Laos' many minorities.[43]

The elections did provide Laos with a potentially neutralist government. Royalists held the majority in the National Assembly. Pro-West diplomat Phoui Sananikone won a slim 29-21 victory to become Premier. The minority Pathet Lao held 13 of 59 seats, a smaller proportion of seats than held by Communists serving in the French and Italian parliaments at that same time.[44] Sananikone's first declaration to the assembly quickly shed the new government's neutralist skin. He pledged his government to "the struggle without fail against the implantation of the Communist ideology in Laos." His cabinet included four members of the far right Committee for the Defense of National Interests (CDNI). Souvanna Phouma, temporarily appointed Ambassador to France, remarked that "the policy of strict neutrality was abandoned under pressure by the United States and replaced by an openly pro-American position." By undermining the policies of the neutralist Souvanna Phouma, the Americans polarized the political climate and actually contributed to the appeal and strength of the Pathet Lao.

In the northern highlands, relative peace followed the departure of the French. Hmong soldiers returned to their farms, hiding their weapons for future use. Opposing camps directed their energies toward the political struggle. Lo Faydang, as Vice-President of the NLHS, became a leading figure in the growing Pathet Lao movement. Touby Lyfoung and his brother, Toulia Lyfoung,

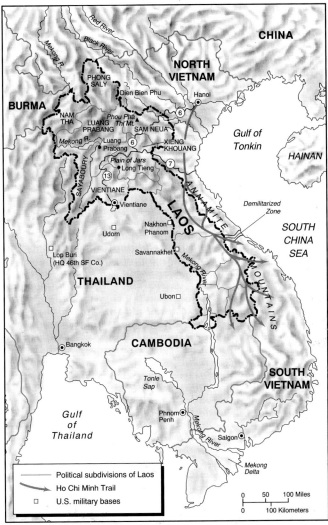

Vietnam's long, mountainous border with Laos was the key to military operations in Southeast Asia. U.S. bombers, based in Thailand, received bearings from the radar installation at Phou Pha Thi for targets in North Vietnam and along the Ho Chi Minh Trail. Hmong soldiers guarded Phou Pha Thi, monitored the trail, and interrupted supplies along Routes 6 and 7. Long Tieng served as headquarters. Map by Carto-Graphics.

won national assembly seats in the 1958 elections. They were joined in Vientiane by NLHS candidate Lo Foung Pablia.[45]

On February 11, 1959, Premier Sananikone stated that he considered "application of the Geneva Agreements as fully accomplished and that, therefore, Laos was no longer bound by its provisions." The Pathet Lao and North Vietnamese saw this as one more sign that the Americans intended to increase their military build-up in Laos. Wholly funded and equipped by the Americans, the Royal Lao Army (RLA) now numbered 25,000, far exceeding a level needed to maintain domestic order. The unnecessarily large force promoted Laotian insecurity by upsetting the 1954 status quo.[46]

Fortified bunkers along the Ho Chi Minh Trail system protected communist soldiers from aerial assaults, ca. 1960s. Timothy Castle. Hmong road watch teams took this and numerous other photos along the trail, which ranged from a two lane road to an invisible jungle path.

Despite American military equipment and training, the RLA showed little ability or inclination to challenge Pathet Lao positions. Graft and patronage plagued both the government and military. In the spring of 1959, the government pressured remaining Pathet Lao units to integrate into the RLA as per the Geneva Accords, but the elusive rebels easily escaped. Sananikone responded by jailing Souphanouvong and other NLHS members of the National Assembly. In July, successful pin-prick attacks against RLA posts in Sam Neua triggered panic in Vientiane. The Sananikone government appealed for international aid against what it described as a massive Vietnamese invasion. Subsequent investigation by a United Nations commission found little evidence for such claims, but in the interim, the charges were widely reported by the American press. Such reports confirmed widespread misimpressions that the conflict in Laos was the result of Vietnamese communist aggression, rather than a civil war escalated, in part, by flawed American policies.[47]

In December 1959, Premier Sananikone attempted to remove Brigadier General Phoumi Nosavan and other CDNI members from his cabinet to reduce the growing influence of the staunchly anti-communist Lao right wing. Phoumi responded by deposing Sananikone in a military coup. Kou Abhay, a Phoumi supporter, became prime minister, and the new government scheduled national elections in April. As in 1958, the elections were marred by widespread fraud. Royalists redrew voting districts to favor their candidates, and raised candidacy educational requirements to disqualify many in the opposition. U.S. embassy personnel observed CIA agents handing out bags of money to village headmen.[48] In Sam Neua Province, a Pathet Lao stronghold, the NLHS candidate received only 13 of 6,521 votes. Royalist candidates won an estimated 90 percent of votes nationwide.

A month after the election, Souphanouvong and other Pathet Lao prisoners escaped with their guards. The country inched one step closer to war. At the same time, North Vietnamese leaders realized that the promised elections to re-unify their country would never be held. They once more prepared for armed liberation. They began by securing border villages, consolidating their positions along the trail system (known collectively as the Ho Chi Minh Trail) that wove through the Annamite Mountains separating Laos from Vietnam. The journey on foot from North Vietnam through Laos to South Vietnam took two months.[49]

A bizarre turn of events in August 1960 illustrates the complexity of Laotian internal politics and why a reading of the conflict in purely Cold War ideological terms was grossly inadequate. Captain Kong Le, an able RLA commander, grew exasperated with widespread corruption and foreign interference. He ordered his battalion of paratroopers to seize control of Vientiane and establish a "truly neutralist government" under Souvanna Phouma. The coup met little initial resistance. In fact, Kong Le was immediately hailed in the streets of Vientiane as a hero. Nearly everyone was caught off guard. American State Department and Intelligence officials debated whom to back. Souvanna Phouma was recognized as a superior leader with broad support in Laos. Yet his willingness to include communists in his government worried the Americans. General Phoumi, although not a U.S. puppet, took a staunchly anti-communist position. However, CIA operatives questioned his leadership ability and noted his narrow base of support.[50]

After an initial wait-and-see reaction, the United States suspended cash-grant aid to Souvanna and backed General Phoumi. With U.S. assistance, Phoumi's forces invaded Vientiane and drove Kong Le's troops northward. At the Plain of Jars, Kong Le made an uneasy alliance with the Pathet Lao. As President Eisenhower prepared to leave the White House in December 1960, he briefed President-elect Kennedy on the tense situation. The Soviet Union was airlifting supplies to Kong Le on the Plain of Jars while the United States continued to back General Phoumi. Both sides defended their actions under the guise of protecting Laotian sovereignty, and accused the other of aiding a rebel force. Eisenhower re-affirmed his view that Laos remained the key to Southeast Asia, and that if necessary, the U.S. should "intervene unilaterally."[5] The conflict assumed catastophic dimensions.

*Above right: **Rightist General Phoumi Nosavan deployed tanks** to drive Kong Le's neutralist forces out of Vientiane, December 17, 1960. AP/Wide World Photos. Below right: **General Kong Le (right) speaks to his officers** at his mountain command post at Ban Na, on the edge of the Plain of Jars, May 27, 1964. UPI/Bettmann.*

I asked General Vang Pao, "Why do you want us to go to war?" Vang Pao replied " ... We are going to war because the North Vietnamese have bombed South Vietnam where the CIA is. I have promised to help the Americans attack Route 7 so that the North Vietnamese cannot cross over to South Vietnam. Everything - supplies, weapons, and money - the Americans will supply me. When the Americans win in South Vietnam, they will help us rebuild our country ... If we help the Americans fight the war and they lose, and we get trouble - cannot live in Laos - they are willing to find a place for us to live."

Chia Koua Xiong
Eau Claire, November 5, 1992
Interviewer: Smidchei Xiong
Translator: Pao Lee

Hmong recruits receive final briefing *before departing on an operation, Xieng Khouang Province, ca. 1961-63. Lloyd "Pat" Landry Papers, McDermott Library, University of Texas - Dallas. Early recruits received training at Phou Vieng, Padong, Pha Khao, Ban Na, Ta Lin Noi, Houie Sa An, as well as specialty training at Hua Hin, Thailand.*

Recruiting the Hmong for a Secret War

President Kennedy spent much of the first months of his presidency sifting through often conflicting advice from insiders in Vientiane and Washington. Unlike Vietnam, Laos was landlocked, and while the possibility of direct U.S. military intervention was discussed, the option was heavily laden with diplomatic and strategic baggage. Such a policy would be an overt violation of the 1954 Geneva Accords. The maintenance of a U.S. force of sufficient size in northern Laos would be logistically difficult and extremely expensive. The U.S. Joint Chiefs of Staff opposed direct intervention, noting that it would require a force of at least 60,000 troops with air support, including the possible use of nuclear weapons.[52] Intervention on that scale might provoke the Chinese, as it had in Korea, or worse, unleash war with the Soviet Union.

Kennedy concluded that America would make its stand in Vietnam, not Laos, but that Laos had to be neutralized. To that end, he shifted American support from General Phoumi back to Souvanna Phouma, whom he believed had broader Laotian support and had previously demonstrated his ability to assemble a neutralist coalition. Kennedy also flexed American muscles, sending the U.S. 7th Fleet to stand by in the South China Sea and placing Okinawa-based troops on alert status. By raising the stakes, he hoped to demonstrate American resolve to the Soviets and move both sides to the negotiating table.[53]

Kennedy also concluded that the ineffective Royal Laotian Army was never going to serve U.S. interests in Laos. He directed U.S. Special Forces to expand the covert program, initiated under President Eisenhower, to recruit and train Lao highlanders, in particular, the Hmong of Xieng Khouang Province. Kennedy ordered the transfer of 16 U.S. Marine Corps H-34 helicopters to the CIA for use by its airline, Air America. At Udorn, Thailand, just 50 miles south of Vientiane, 300 members of Task Force 116 began setting up a helicopter repair and maintenance base. American military advisors in Laos, who had previously operated as "civilians" under the Programs Evaluation Office, now conducted their activities openly as an official Military Assistance Advisory Group or MAAG.[54]

The Hmong had a reputation as good fighters. They were alarmed by the proximity of Kong Le's troops on the Plain of Jars, but were not anxious to aid the lowland Lao who often treated them with contempt. Lloyd "Pat" Landry, John "Jack" Shirley, and James "Bill" Lair were among the first team of CIA case officers sent in to recruit the Hmong in 1959. They argued that if the Hmong did not fight, the North Vietnamese would come to take their land. They promised that the United States would provide arms and supplies, and that in victory or defeat, the Americans would take care of them. This promised commitment by the Americans did not constitute a formal treaty and was never written down, yet years later, it would be recalled by countless Hmong who had fled Laos as a result of the war.[55]

To lead the Hmong force, CIA operatives recruited Lieutenant Colonel Vang Pao, at that time the only Hmong to achieve a commission in the Royal Lao Army. A native of Xieng Khouang province, Vang Pao had gained his early military experience fighting with the French in Touby Lyfoung's militia. Through the intercession of French commander Captain Fiet, he attended Dong Hene officers' school in southern Laos, receiving his commission in March 1952. Two years later, he led 850 commandos on a forced march through the rugged mountains of Sam Neua in a vain attempt to relieve the French garrison at Dien Bien Phu.[56] In 1960, his reputation as a commander impressed the

Air America pilot Fred Sass poses at Houei 7 with General Vang Pao, 1961. Fred Sass Papers, McDermott Library, University of Texas - Dallas. Sass later wrote that Vang Pao "had bags full of money to pay the troops, they all look a little impatient in the background."

*Above: **The Plain of Jars**, March 1970. Photographer: Leslie W. Bays, Air America pilot. The wide grassy plain, littered with ancient earthen funerary jars, has historically served as a crossroads for commerce and route for invading armies. Below: **Grenade-throwing training at Phou Vieng**, ca. 1961-63. Lloyd "Pat" Landry Papers. Both at McDermott Library, University of Texas - Dallas.*

Americans. For the next 15 years he would act as commander of Military Region II, the strategic area surrounding the Plain of Jars, achieving the rank of General.

Vang Pao's controversial leadership of the Hmong during the war has since garnered him praise and criticism. In *Tragic Mountains*, author Jane Hamilton-Merritt exalted his skill as a military tactician. "Vang Pao's canny — seemingly omniscient — understanding of his enemy mystified his American advisors." She described him as a charismatic personality, "of seemingly indomitable spirit and boundless energy," a man entirely devoted to the cause of his people.[57] Historian Alfred McCoy took a more critical view. He noted that Touby Lyfoung had succeeded by carefully managing his relationship with the French so as to exact the maximum benefit for the Hmong without putting his troops in a position to take heavy casualties. Unlike Touby, Vang Pao was willing to suffer enormous casualties for dubious military objectives which in the end left his supporters vulnerable. In a 1971 interview, Touby Lyfoung told McCoy: "He is a pure military officer who doesn't understand that after the war there is peace. And one must be strong to win the peace."[58]

To gain legitimacy, Vang Pao allied himself closely with Touby Lyfoung, then Minister for Social Welfare, the first Hmong to achieve a cabinet level post in the Vientiane government. Accompanied by CIA case officers, including skilled linguist William Young, Vang Pao flew from village to village enlisting the support of local *tassengs* and *naibans*. Their ability to recruit soldiers through kinship and village loyalties was essential. The *tassengs* grudgingly gave their support, but reminded Vang Pao of the wounds of the previous war and the sudden French departure. They urged him to proceed cautiously in his dealings with the Americans.[59]

When fighting broke out on the Plain of Jars in December 1960, Vang Pao initiated the evacuation of some 200 Hmong villages to seven pre-selected "safe" mountain sites ringing the Plain of Jars. The American strategy was to keep the Pathet Lao bottled up on the Plain by recruiting Hmong in the surrounding mountains to launch guerrilla attacks on communist positions. Vang Pao set up his headquarters south of the Plain at Padong and Air America delivered food and arms. From Padong, he commanded troops as far north as Phou Fa, and as far east as Bouam Long.[60] (See map, page 44.)

The evacuation strategy succeeded in training and equipping about 5,000 Hmong troops, but failed to make adequate provision for some 70,000 villagers driven from their rice fields by the fighting. In the ensuing months, many died from starvation or disease as a result of malnutrition. International Voluntary Service volunteer Edgar "Pop" Buell spearheaded relief efforts by the U.S. Agency for International Development (USAID), delivering food and medicine to the Hmong refugees. The rescue effort evolved into an integral part of the American war effort.Using Air America transport, USAID dispatched food, clothing, medicine, and other supplies to soldiers, their families, and thousands of refugees displaced by the war. The arrangement was both practical and diplomatic, creating a scenario of "plausible deniability" in which Americans masked illegal military operations under the guise of humanitarian relief.[61]

By March 1961, the Pathet Lao held territory in six provinces, defined as "liberated zones." Vang Pao's soldiers fought fiercely at Padong. They managed to hold out until June against larger, better equipped forces. In the meantime, President Kennedy succeeded in bringing about a second Geneva peace conference. As in 1954, the 1962 Geneva Accords guaranteed Laotian neutrality, prohibited foreign troops on Laotian soil and foreign military assistance beyond the needs of the Royal Lao government for internal security. As in 1954, the Accords failed to stop the escalating conflict. The Americans and North Vietnamese were moving toward a violent confrontation in Vietnam. Neither was willing to concede the strategic advantages offered by Laos. North Vietnamese troops remained in northeastern Laos, and the CIA continued secretly supplying the Hmong.[62] Unlike the 1954 agreement, the United States was an official party to the 1962 agreements and legally bound by them. For that reason, American military activities in Laos after 1962 remained secret. Instead of using U.S. military officers, the White House relied upon CIA case officers to maintain operations because of their "plausible deniability." Air America advertised itself as a private, independent airline, and its pilots carried nothing that could be used to link them to the U.S. government. American officials publicly denied any covert operations in Laos until 1969 when growing anti-war sentiment made it politically feasible for the Senate Committee on Foreign Affairs to hold oversight hearing.[63]

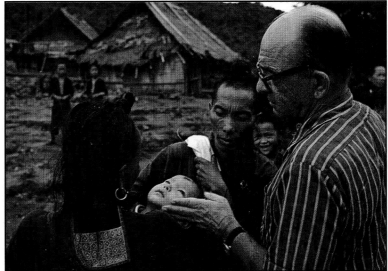

*Above: **Air America "kickers" air dropping sacks of rice**, ca. 1971-72. Allen Rich Papers, McDermott Library, University of Texas - Dallas. Below: **Refugee aid worker "Pop" Buell examines a child** stricken with dengue fever, Phu Pha Daeng, May-July 1973. Photographer: W.E. Garrett, ©National Geographic Society.*

Long Tieng, General Vang Pao's military headquarters, grew from a small village to the second largest city in Laos with more than 50,000 residents, mostly soldiers and their families, ca. 1968-69. Capt. David Kouba, CASI.

... [After breakfast] at the airport in Vientiane ... you'd go out, preflight your airplane, and ... find out where you were going .... You might have to go up to Lima Site 5, a 45-minute flight. The kicker would tie down the load and you'd fly over there and they might say they had some wounded for Sam Thong. Then you'd fly a few people back to Long Tieng, where they'd give you some ammunition to drop at Lima 32. You couldn't go there direct because the bad guys had guns over the PDJ (Plain of Jars) [sic] so you had to go around .... By this time it might be noon. You'd drop the ammo off with parachutes .... then you might take some troops over to Lima 14 and bring some back, relieving an outpost .... Then we'd fly back to Long Tieng, pick up some rice, and drop it free fall to some little outpost .... [Altogether, on an average day] 8-10 hours of flying.

William Leinbach
Air America Pilot
(Robbins, *Air America*, 106-07)

The Secret Army and Monsoon Warfare

By the spring of 1962, Vang Pao had established a major base southwest of the Plain of Jars at Long Tieng. His troop strength had grown to approximately 14,000 - 18,000 men, mostly Hmong but also including Yao, Khmu, and Thai soldiers. Selected troops were sent to training camps in Thailand to learn vital skills in artillery and explosives, as well as map reading and radio communications. Regular Air America flights to Long Tieng from Vientiane and Udorn, Thailand, brought rice, equipment, and "hard rice" (ammunition). Long Tieng became the forward-staging area for American-supported Hmong operations in northern Laos. Nineteen miles away at Sam Thong, USAID established a headquarters for refugee relief and care of the wounded.

At its peak, more than 50,000 people, mostly soldiers and their families, resided at Long Tieng, making it the second largest city in Laos. Long Tieng's paved runway was banked on either side by temporary "neighborhoods" of refugee housing. A large open air market became a major trading center for goods traveling back and forth from Vientiane. Villagers, unable to farm, became adept at selling everything from rice and fresh vegetables, to rubber bands and Pepsi. Near the end of the runway, General Vang Pao ordered the construction of a Buddhist temple to appease Lao fears about Hmong secessionist intentions. In fact, the possibility of an independent state was used by Vang Pao to obtain Hmong support for the war, exploiting folklore which predicted that an ancient king would return to establish a Hmong kingdom.[64]

Hmong draftees were nicknamed "carbine soldiers" because many were no taller than their M-1 rifles. They fought a guerrilla war against the Pathet Lao and North Vietnamese designed to halt communist advances in Laos while assisting U.S. military efforts in Vietnam. Vang Pao organized his forces along two lines: regional platoons and companies assigned local tasks and strike forces called Special Guerilla Units (SGUs) for major offensive or defensive purposes. The war's tactics were determined, to a large extent, by the geography and climate of the region. North Vietnamese and Pathet Lao forces attacked during the winter dry season when truck convoys could haul their heavy artillery along gravel roads. From June to October, when monsoon rains turned those roads to mud, the Hmong counter-attacked. They relied on their knowledge and ability to operate in the mountainous terrain, striking quickly and withdrawing.[65]

American, Laotian and a few Hmong pilots, dubbed "sky" by Hmong soldiers, greatly improved troop mobility and provided fire power for Hmong missions. Air America pilots transported troops and supplies to hundreds of crude airstrips located throughout northeastern Laos. The airstrips, known as "Lima Sites," were often no more than a dirt swath cleared by local villagers who removed the largest rocks and hand-tamped the ground. Some sites ran up the sides of steep slopes or dog-legged in the middle. Air America used small STOL (short take-off and landing) aircraft, such as the Helio Courier and the PC-6 Pilatus Porter, that could easily navigate through jagged mountain peaks and land on tiny airstrips.[66] Lima Sites became an important component of the Hmong "trip-wire," used both to gather information and ambush enemy soldiers. Hmong soldiers frequently depended on air support, and reciprocated by risking their own lives to save downed pilots.

Road watch team members Thao Pao Vue, with field telephone, and Yee Vue, holding RPG-2 rocket launcher, outside Long Tieng, 1972. Thao Pao Vue.

To gather intelligence for U.S. bombing runs along the Ho Chi Minh Trail, small Hmong units, called "road watch" teams, infiltrated communist positions. In some places the trail appeared as wide as a city street, in others the dense foliage nearly swallowed it up. Road watch teams monitored troop movements along the trail and the number and types of vehicles. They used still and movie cameras to provide accurate intelligence on enemy activity. They also set up boobytraps and ambushes and used field telephones to call in air strikes. Such efforts hampered but did not halt the steady flow of troops and materiel to the south.[67]

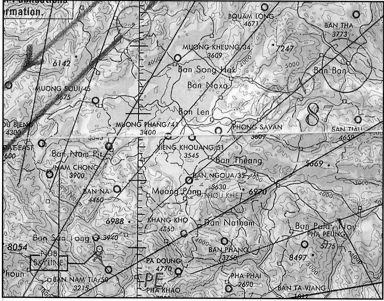

Hmong soldiers also guarded radar installations which guided U.S. fighter bombers on missions in northern Laos and Vietnam. The 5,800 foot-high Phou Pha Thi mountain ridge provided an excellent site, located just 20 miles from North Vietnam and overlooking Routes 6 and 7, the two major highways in the region. The Americans installed a Tactical Air Navigation System in 1966, and a TSQ 81 radar bomb facility in mid-1967. The installation could guide U.S. aircraft to targets within 60 miles of Hanoi regardless of the weather. While it was in operation over the next two years, U.S. Air Force bombers dropped more than 350,000 tons of bombs in Laos and another 500,000 tons in Vietnam.[68]

The North Vietnamese and Pathet Lao recognized the importance of the site and organized numerous attacks. One extremely steep ridge of the mountain was mined. Hmong troops guarded the more accessible route with 105mm and 155mm guns, and a host of smaller weapons. American and Thai technicians on top could easily call in air strikes at first sign of attack. On March 11, 1968, while their heavy artillery bombarded the troops below, the communists used lightweight mine detectors and scaled the steep slope unnoticed.

U.S. Air Force and Air America helicopters were called to the scene, but not before the site was overrun and Hmong, Thai, and American lives lost. For two weeks, the U.S. Air Force repeatedly bombed the site to destroy any remaining equipment. In November, Vang Pao deployed 5,000 troops in a final attempt to retake the strategic site. He established a forward headquarters two miles south at Houei Ma, and persuaded some 6,000 refugees in the area to remain for fear of what a general evacuation would do to the morale of his troops. Despite continued strafing by Lao T-28 propeller planes and U.S. jets, the Hmong were unable to gain a foothold on the peak. The battle raged continuously for 27 days, when the General ordered his troops to withdraw to Na Khang. He had lost more than 300 men.[69]

... men with weapons of all sizes attacked each other ferociously; airplanes strafing the jungle turned everything to confusion, killing the animals and destroying the trees. When we began we had eight companies. Company Six's first Platoon had only 14 survivors. B.V. 27 [Laotian] lost 40 men. B.V. 29 lost 60. B.V. 28 lost 250 .... After that, the Vietnamese Communists came to attack us. We ... fought each other

Above: **Looking down** *on the slight, bowed air strip at Lima Site 337. Robert M. Hifler Papers, McDermott Library, University of Texas-Dallas. Wind socks were unreliable on such strips because villagers, realizing that pilots would not land if the socks were blowing, put rocks in them. Below:* **Pilot's map.** *By November 1972, an estimated 450 Lima Sites (shown as small circles) dotted northern Laos.*

intensely for 3 days and 3 nights .... We began the attack with each man behind a huge boulder. If I throw a grenade and it goes over the rock, he dies; but if I throw it, and it doesn't go over, I die. Our fighting on Pha Thee kept us from eating. One canteen of water had to last you a week. ... you were so thirsty that you couldn't even summon spit to wet your mouth.

Tong Pao Xiong
Interview in La Crosse (WI) , 1993
(Hmong Lives, 155-57)

Fighting Next to Family

The soldiers come a lot [to Sam Thong], and we so scared and we ask them and they say, "The communist is there." So we just run, ... Don't take anything .... [Pa Foua] was just two years old and I was pregnant 8 months .... We went to the farm where my parents lived .... It was very hard, everybody come, all the people .... We were so scared to walk in the street, the little trail, we just go through the jungle ... because we heard the noise, the bombs, start to hear the guns, you know - boom, boom, boom, boom, boom. We ran for half a day .... We went through the jungle and I fell so many times, and I felt that my baby moved down, and my mom so scared that we going to lose the baby ...

Mai Xao Yang
Madison (WI), August 22, 1994
Interviewer: Tim Pfaff

Most Hmong viewed the war not in ideological terms, but as a fight for their homes. Villagers came under intense pressure from both sides to join their cause. Local neutrality, like national neutrality, became difficult to maintain. With many villages located within communist controlled territory, soldiers battled in firefights that could be seen and heard by nearby relatives. Families repeatedly abandoned fields for "safe" areas, fleeing along narrow mountain trails under cover of darkness. They sought shelter in limestone caves to escape aerial bombardments, and hid in thick bamboo stands to avoid enemy patrols.

By 1969 more than 110,000 Hmong had become refugees in their own country, settling southwest of the Plain of Jars. From Sam Thong, Pop Buell coordinated USAID's refugee relief program. Air America parachuted rice, medicine, salt, blankets, and even live pigs to waiting families who could no longer support themselves. Children growing up in a decade of war knew more about rice "from the sky" than from the field. Flattened oil drums, burlap sacks and plastic tarps became

Living in the midst of war, May-July 1973. W.E. Garrett, ©National Geographic Society. Intense aerial bombardment drove thousands of refugees southward away from the Plain of Jars.

*Above: **Rice from the sky**, August 1971. Alfred W. McCoy. Unable to farm, refugees depended on air supply for survival. Below: **Refugee housing at Muong Soui** included plastic tarps, empty rice sacks and fuel drums, 1970. Dan Williams.*

building materials for temporary shelters. Teachers called students with school bells made from bomb shell casings. For more than a decade, families went on with their lives filled with extraordinary risks and uncertainty about the future.

Expanding War and Mounting Casualties

The bombs! The bombs! Every [Hmong] village north of here [pointing to the northeast] has been bombed .... There are big holes in every village. Every house is destroyed. If bombs didn't hit some houses, they were burned. Everything is gone. Everything from this village all the way up to Muong Soui and all of Xieng Khouang [Plain of Jars] is destroyed. In Xieng Khouang there are bomb craters .. all over the plain. Every village in Xieng Khouang has been bombed, and many, many people died.

Ger Su Yang
Long Pot Village, August 1971
*(McCoy, **Politics of Heroin** ... 292)*

The loss of Phou Pha Thi in the spring of 1969 came as a strategic and psychological blow. For Vang Pao, it was personal loss of face. The North Vietnamese capitalized on the victory by stepping up troop movements through Laos. Vang Pao responded by ordering a controversial offensive on the Plain of Jars, dubbed "Operation About Face." [70] The Pathet Lao and North Vietnamese had long used the Plain as a staging area. Their tanks and heavy artillery could be employed more easily on the broad, flat plain.

Some of the General's CIA advisors supported the plan, while others objected to the use of a guerilla army for a conventional battle. Years of bloodshed had taken a heavy toll on Vang Pao's forces. Many village leaders were unwilling or unable to supply more soldiers. A year before, Pop Buell speculated that out of 300 new recruits, 30 percent were less than 14 and 40 percent were 45 or older. [71]

Operation About Face, unleashed in September near the end of the monsoons, caught the Communists by surprise. Hmong soldiers swept across the Plain and confiscated huge caches of guns and ammunition. As CIA advisors feared, however, the Secret Army was not well-suited for holding territory. The North Vietnamese and Pathet Lao launched a tank-led counterattack in January 1970. Despite massive aerial bombardment, including for the first time strikes by U.S. B-52s, the Communists drove Vang Pao's forces from the Plain. In March, Sam Thong was overrun and Long Tieng's "skyline ridge" came under fire. Pop Buell relocated his crew to Ban Xon, trailed by more than 8,000 refugees. Vang Pao's forces suffered heavy casualties, but managed to hold out until monsoon rains forced the enemy to withdraw.

Tragically, this scenario was repeated again beginning in May 1971 when Vang Pao launched "Operation About Face II." Once again, the battle pitted superior North Vietnamese long-range artillery against American air power. Again, the Secret Army was able to capture the Plain of Jars, but six months later retreated to Long Tieng. Again, Vang Pao's forces suffered heavy casualties. As a result, much of northeastern Laos was littered with bomb craters. On several occasions, American officials suspended bombing campaigns in North Vietnam to appease anti-war activists, yet in reality, the bombing just shifted to Laos where it was not widely reported. In a war without fronts and battle lines, such aerial assaults failed to distinguish between enemy and ally, between soldier and civilian.

By 1972, the war had claimed more than 10,000 Hmong soldiers, and perhaps twice as many civilians. Boys as young as 10 were drafted to fight. Unable to draft sufficient Hmong soldiers, the CIA began shoring up the ranks with Thai mercenaries. Long Tieng and Ban Xon overflowed with refugees. After their annual spring offensive, the communists withdrew only a day's march from Long Tieng. Vang Pao's counterattack went no further than the southwest corner of the Plain before it was met by enemy tanks.[72]

In the meantime, U.S. National Security Advisor Henry Kissinger began secret negotiations with North Vietnamese Foreign Minister Le Duc Tho. The war in Laos, as it had since 1961, took a backseat to American policy in Vietnam. The talks set the stage for the U.S. withdrawal from Southeast Asia. On January 27, 1973, the two signed the Paris Agreement on Ending the War and Restoring Peace in Vietnam. In Article 20, each agreed to "strictly respect" the 1962 Geneva Agreements on Laos.[73]

*Above: **Hmong ranks suffered heavy casualties** trying to hold the Plain of Jars, ca. 1970-71. Below: **Mounting casualties forced General Vang Pao to recruit boys** as young as 10 for battle, ca. 1970-71. Papers of Allen Rich, McDermott Library, University of Texas - Dallas.*

Living on the run, *Xieng Khouang Province, 1970. Photographer: Wayne Persons. Hmong families drifted from one "safe" area to another until 1975 when the American withdrawal triggered a mass exodus to Thailand.*

Chapter III: Exodus to Thailand

The American withdrawal in 1975 created panic and chaos throughout Southeast Asia as hundreds of thousands of refugees from South Vietnam, Laos, and Cambodia fled to Thailand. Those who had aided the Americans feared that they would be targeted for revenge once the Communists came to power. Others fled the staggering devastation that years of bombing and bloodshed had heaped upon their homelands.

To no one's surprise, the American withdrawal spelled the end of the Royal Lao Government. A provisional coalition government, formed in 1974, provided a face-saving transition to Pathet Lao rule. Deprived of the American subsidies upon which it had grown dependent for more than a decade, the Laotian economy collapsed. Cut off from American arms and air power, the Secret Army disbanded. In May 1975, General Vang Pao and many of his supporters were airlifted from Long Tieng to Thailand. Thousands followed on foot. Others remained to rebuild their homes and villages or continue the fight. From 1975 through 1992, more than 100,000 Hmong crossed into Thailand, along with nearly 250,000 ethnic Lao and other Laotian highlanders. Approximately 200,000 Hmong remained in Laos.

South of the Mekong River in Thailand, refugees poured into crude, overcrowded camps with food and water in short supply. Malnutrition and disease in the confined spaces produced many deaths. Within months, the United Nations High Commissioner on Refugees (UNHCR) and a host of international agencies responded to the crisis, coordinating food, water, housing, and medical supplies. Over time, conditions improved. The camps developed a culture of their own with schools, markets and recognized leaders. Nevertheless, the camps remained temporary as refugees pondered the inevitable — whether to return to Laos, or pursue life in another country.

The first day ... C-130 transport planes flew back and forth between Long Tieng and Thailand .... As we boarded the plane, people kept boarding even after the plane was too full .... I had to push some off to make sure the plane would take off. Angry people, who didn't have a chance to get on the plane, shot their guns at the sky. Those who were on the plane were so crowded that they stepped on a woman and she screamed for help, but no one would help until I came and started to push people away, to pull her out from people's feet. When I got into Thailand, I still carried my hand-gun and had my police uniform on.

Fatong Vang
Eau Claire, May 15, 1991
Interview and translation:
Charles Vue and Kao Xiong

Refugees crowded around cargo planes at Long Tieng, *seeking to escape to Thailand, May 1975. Allen Rich Papers, McDermott Library, University of Texas - Dallas. Widespread fear of communist reprisals produced panic when the Americans pulled out.*

Fleeing Laos

After the signing of the Paris peace agreement between the United States and the North Vietnamese in 1973, Henry Kissinger flew to Vientiane where he pressured the Laotian Prime Minister to accept a similar arrangement. Souvanna Phouma had little choice. The Agreement on the Restoration of Peace and Reconciliation in Laos called for an end to hostilities and the creation of a government of national union. Its language resembled the earlier Geneva Accords, yet the reality of the imminent American pullout cast a lingering shadow. The agreement established a cease-fire line and required "the withdrawal of foreign military personnel, regular and irregular" from Laos. "Special Forces," defined as those "organized, trained, equipped and controlled by foreigners" were to be disbanded. General Vang Pao maintained his command at Long Tieng, but was ordered to integrate his forces into the Royal Lao Army.[74]

Laotians greeted the truce with a mixture of hope and distrust. Hmong made up 70 percent of the 155,474 refugees in Xieng Khouang Province, and 32 percent of the 370,000 Laotian people who had become dependent on government support as a result of the war. Well-known *naikongs* Kia Pao Kue, Chia Koua Kha and Xiong Pao Ly led groups of refugees to virgin lands in the area surrounding Long Tieng to resume farming. Touby Lyfoung, Yang Dao, Lyteck Ly Nhia Vue, and other Hmong officials in the new provisional government cooperated in plans for the country's postwar recovery.[75]

Without U.S. military interference, it was only a matter of time before the Pathet Lao assumed control of the government. Pathet Lao leaders began replacing Royalists in key cabinet positions. In the spring of 1975, organized Pathet Lao protesters in Vientiane spewed angry, anti-American rhetoric. Defying the Vientiane Agreement, North Vietnamese troops followed up victories in South Vietnam and Cambodia with attacks against Royal Lao Army positions along the cease-fire line. When Vang Pao ordered the remaining T-28s at his disposal to strike communist positions, he was rebuffed by Souvanna Phouma. After a heated meeting between the two on May 6, Vang Pao angrily resigned his commission and returned to Long Tieng.[76]

The provisional government announced soon after that Vang Pao would be replaced as commander of Military Region II. On May 10, General Harry C. Aderholt dispatched several C-130 cargo planes to evacuate Vang Pao's supporters from Long Tieng to Nam Phong camp, next to Ubon airbase in Thailand. Vang Pao's imminent departure triggered panic among his supporters. Cargo planes evacuated 12,000-15,000 people, less than half of those swarming the Long Tieng runway. In some cases, pilots had to order passengers off so that their heavily laden aircraft could clear the rocky peaks on takeoff. On May 14, 1975, the fourth and final day of the air evacuation, Vang Pao joined his officers and their families in Thailand.[77]

*Unable to get aboard a plane at Long Tieng, **Kou Yang** fled with his family by jeep to Vientiane, crossed the Mekong to Thailand, and located his missing daughter, Pader, in a refugee camp, ca. 1975. Mai Xao Yang.*

[My husband Kou] said, "Go to the airport .... I will put you in the airplane so that I can stay [and] fight. We tried to get into the airplanes for two days .... we never get inside. When the cargo airplane got down and opened the back, a million people tried to get in there .... We never make it. "The last one," they said, "this is the last one." ... [Kou] told me, "Try to get in there." And everybody tried .... and a lot of people just pushed our back ... just climb over our heads to get inside. [Kou and my daughters] Pa Foua and Pader [climbed up] in the top ... but I was down there ... carrying Youa Pa. My baby-sitter carrying Tony. And the [crowd] ... pushed us down and they step over and over .... We [were] on the floor. My husband think that we going to die. So he jumped back to help us and Pa Foua jumped after him ... but Pader just go straight. Pader didn't jump back .... After he got off ... the airplane start to move away. [Kou] run after and the American people say "Nooo!" ... "My baby is there," he tried to say that, but they say no .... They closed the door and take off .... Pader was 5 years old.

> Mai Xao Yang
> Madison (WI), August 22, 1994
> Interviewer: Tim Pfaff

Those who remained in Laos pursued one of three alternatives. Many hid their weapons, discarded uniforms and other materials that could be used to tie them to the Americans, and attempted to return to village life. Others took refuge in the dense forests, hoping to stay out of harm's way until the political situation improved or they could escape to neighboring Thailand. Thousands fled immediately. Human convoys stretched for miles along the road to Vientiane.[78] From Long Tieng, they headed south to Ban Xon/Na Xou, the last major refugee settlement before Vientiane. Souvanna Phouma tried to stem the tide by ordering Touby Lyfoung to urge refugees to return to their villages. His pleas went unheeded.

On May 29, 1975, an estimated 20,000-30,000 people advanced on the narrow checkpoint at Hin Heup Bridge guarded by Pathet Lao and Neutralist soldiers. When refugees ignored warnings to turn back, soldiers fired into the crowd. News of the incident spread like wildfire, feeding long-held fears about communist reprisals. Desperation took hold. Families butchered livestock for a last meal before their departure. Suicides increased among older people unable to make the journey.[79]

After Hin Heup, the road was soon reopened but many had already taken to the mountains. Some lived off the land, hiding in the jungle for years until they could cross the Mekong River into Thailand. Parents fed crying babies opium to prevent them from alerting communist patrols. At the Mekong, desperate refugees hired Lao and Thai boatmen, used inner tubes, or fashioned crude bamboo rafts. Yang Dao estimated the Hmong population in Laos at approximately 300,000 in 1970. At the end of 1975, the UNHCR estimated that 44,659 Laotian highlanders had crossed into Thailand.[80]

I was only a few miles from Hin Heup. Taxis transported some wounded people back and told us they were being attacked by the Communists. We then returned back to Na Xou. As we got back, we butchered animals for a feast, but the food seemed to taste terrible. Peace was never in our mind. We only thought about fleeing the war and the Communists.

Lia Lee
Eau Claire, May 15, 1991
Interview and translation by:
Charles Vue and Kao Xiong

***Storycloth**, made in Ban Vinai Refugee Camp, northern Thailand, 1988. Science Museum of Minnesota. Storycloths, a new needlework form developed in the camps, often chronicle the Hmong exodus. Here, reading in a z-pattern: Hmong villagers flee enemy soldiers and escape to the jungle where they live in crude shelters. Unable to remain, they cross the Mekong River to reach refugee camps in Thailand. There they apply for resettlement and board buses bound for Bangkok and eventually a flight to the United States.*

Following their surrender to Pathet Lao troops, Hmong and Thai troops are led to detention centers, Spring 1975. Roger Warner.

"Seminar" and Resistance

The victorious Pathet Lao quickly assumed control of the government's defense and internal police forces. They disarmed Royal Lao Government troops and replaced the old political hierarchy with local committees. In December 1975 they officially formed the Lao People's Democratic Republic (LPDR). Lo Faydang became a vice-president of the Supreme People's Assembly, along with other minority leaders. His brother, Nhiavu Lobliayao, was appointed Chairman of the Nationalities Committee.[81] The new government's three-year plan aimed to restore order, repatriate refugees, and rebuild the nation's economy. The latter proved to be the most difficult, and persistent shortages of food, medicine, and other necessities contributed to the ongoing exodus of refugees to Thailand.

To consolidate their hold on the country, the Pathet Lao set up a chain of prison labor camps called "seminar." There, they "re-educated" perceived enemies, targeting former *naibans* and *tassengs*, as well as known military officials and soldiers. The purge aimed to clear the way for new political administrators and reduce the lingering influence of rightists, either in Laos or nearby Thailand. Prisoners, put to hard labor constructing roads and other needed public works, often endured brutal living conditions. Their indefinite sentences ranged from a few months to many years. Those who survived seminar recalled daily political indoctrination sessions where they were required to confess crimes. Touby Lyfoung reportedly died of malaria in Sop Hoa camp in Sam Neua in 1978.[82]

Although their leaders were imprisoned, the majority of the Hmong (and other groups) were allowed and even encouraged to return to their villages. The resulting breakup of families, however, had a chilling effect on the Hmong. Many retrieved their weapons and joined armed resistance groups. Vang Pao's soldiers, numbering about 3,000, conducted missions into Laos from Thai refugee camps. By 1976, the strongest resistance centered around Phou Bia, highest peak in Laos. Sai Shua Yang, a former *tasseng,* drew support from soldiers left behind at Long Tieng. Outnumbered and outgunned, Yang's group conducted hit-and-run raids and ambushes to conserve ammunition.[83]

Zong Zua Heu led a messianic rebel group, the *Chao Fa* (Lord of the Sky). Chao Fa warriors erected temples and conducted mystical ceremonies to protect themselves in combat. Heu drew legitimacy by identifying himself with former Hmong leaders Pa Chai Vue and Shong Lue Yang. Pa Chai Vue had led the 1919 rebellion against the French. He had claimed to be in touch with ancient Hmong kings and revived stories of the mythical Sin Sai who protected people from giants and evil spirits. Shong Lue Yang, an uneducated Hmong farmer, had emerged in the 1960s as a spiritual leader, largely through his development of a Hmong writing system. His teachings revived the Chao Fa during the war, drawing followers from both Lo Faydang and Vang Pao camps. Viewed with suspicion by both sides, he was assassinated in January 1971 by soldiers under Vang Pao's command.[84]

Local security forces proved inadequate to quell Hmong resistance. The government deployed regular army troops. In 1977-78, an estimated 10,000-30,000 Vietnamese and Pathet Lao soldiers launched coordinated attacks against resistance strongholds at Phou Bia. The communist offensive broke the back of the resistance, inflicting heavy Hmong casualties.[85] The numbers of Hmong crossing into Thailand rose from 11,886 in 1977-78 to 38,744 in 1979-80. Survivors reported attacks of "yellow rain" or chemical warfare, an explosive accusation which immediately attracted international media coverage. Journalists wrote of a genocidal campaign against the Hmong, and called for sanctions against the governments of Laos, Vietnam, and the Soviet Union. Some attributed the U.S. government's reluctance to press the issue to its desire to obtain LPDR cooperation on American prisoners-of-war and those missing in action.

In *The Yellow Rainmakers*, author Grant Evans examined U.S. government findings in the report, *Chemical Warfare in Southeast Asia and Afghanistan* (March 1982). He also interviewed Hmong refugees in Thailand as well as villagers in Laos. He concluded that the government's case lacked verifiable scientific data and relied almost entirely on refugee reports. In interviews with those refugees named in the report, he found numerous inconsistencies and was unable to corroborate their stories with those of additional individuals on the scene when the alleged gassings took place. Evans argued that riot control gases and

Chao Fa leader Zong Zua Heu, whose beard was believed to give him magical powers. Kao Xiong.

chemical defoliants had been used against the Hmong resistance. Such gases were commonly used by the Americans during the Vietnam War, and stockpiles had been left behind. He was unable to find evidence confirming the use of chemical toxins. Evans hypothesized that such stories could have been planted to discredit the new Laotian government, draw support for continued resistance, or influence arms control negotiations between the United States and the Soviet Union.

The Mekong River represented a formidable barrier to many refugees who paddled across on inner tubes and makeshift bamboo rafts. View from Pak Chom area, Loei Province, Thailand, 1981. Photographer: Wayne Persons.

In 1982 ... we ran out of bullets .... We [264 people] left Tha Vieng and departed for the Mekong River. On the way ... the Vietnamese killed five of our people - one was my son, three were my nephews, and one was a Her family member. [We] had eaten all the food we had carried. .... We cut bamboo to make rafts .... [and] waited until dusk .... When all the people were ready, we paddled to Thailand. We arrived at Pa Sa, Thailand at 5:00 a.m. .... Some of our people got sick. The Thai people who lived along the river brought us food. As a human being, struggling like that was the lowest life on this earth.

Chia Koua Xiong
Eau Claire, November 5, 1992
Interviewer: Smidchei Xiong
Translator: Pao Lee

Crowded into Refugee Camps

The initial flood of refugees overwhelmed border villages in Thailand. Within months, camps for arriving Laotians were hastily set up at Nong Khai, Nam Yao, Ban Vinai, and Loei. Those who had earlier been airlifted to Nam Phong were transferred to Ban Vinai. Set up to accommodate 12,000 people, in July 1979 Ban Vinai was bursting with 42,000. In the camps, two or three families typically shared a bamboo hut 10-feet square, cooking collectively over charcoal pots and sleeping in shifts.[86] Refugees arrived with few belongings. Having bribed river boatmen or Thai patrols to cross the border, they quickly exhausted

[At Nong Khai in 1976], there were 12,000 of us and we lived in a very small space. People slept one on top of the other .... There was no shelter when we got there, so we just dug a small gutter around our sleeping place and put a blanket down to sleep on. We put a small tent over us so that the rain did not come down on us .... It was easier to earn a dollar than to earn a gallon of water .... Because of the shortage of food and water, we developed rashes all over our bodies .... Everyday about six people died in the camp.

Touly Xiong
Eau Claire, June 1991
Interviewer: Charles Vang

Waiting for water in the sweltering heat of crowded Ban Vinai Refugee Camp, ca. 1983-85. Photographer: Jan Folsom.

remaining cash on food, shelter and other necessities. Although UNHCR provided subsistence food, water, and shelter for most of the refugees, some hired out as laborers in local Thai forests and rice paddies, risking being robbed on their way in and out of camp. Women and children greeted the morning with tin pails and metal cans, waiting in long lines for the day's ration of water.

In 1976, Hmong funeral drums beat continuously at Ban Vinai.[87] From every corner of the camp, at any time of day, *qeej* musicians guided departed souls to meet their ancestors. Serious overcrowding, poor sanitation, and malnutrition created ideal conditions for disease. Unaccustomed to the sweltering temperatures of the lowlands, many Hmong contracted malaria. As a doctor at Ban Vinai in 1979, Mace Goldfarb

Mourning the dead at Ban Vinai Refugee Camp, 1982. Photographer: Wayne Persons. Hmong funeral ceremonies required that a qeej *player guide the soul of the departed back to its ancestors.*

treated numerous patients suffering from tuberculosis, pneumonia, diarrhea, and skin infections.[88] It was a time of great sorrow.

Medical facilities consisted of a series of barracks-like buildings. Patients awaited treatment on rows of hard wooden pallets with wicker mats. A small lab analyzed blood and urine samples, but more sophisticated tests or x-rays were out of the question. Former military officers, clan elders, and village leaders organized the Hmong into sections, with leaders reporting to a camp commander. Doctors worked through the network of Hmong leaders to dispense immunizations. Herbalists gathered local plants for home remedies. Shamans erected signposts to lure back the spirits of victims.[89]

Noob ncoos (*funeral square*), *Blue/Green Hmong, ca. 1983. Elizabeth Perkins. Made by daughters or daughters-in-law and used as a pillow covering, designs represent house and fields, assuring property in the future life. Grid designs represent the interlocking arms and legs of clan relatives, past and present.*

At the very beginning when Hmong people die, they have to give her or him some new clothes to wear and wash the body .... The qeej *players have to play ... a certain song ... The Hmong people believe, if you die, your body is dead but you have many spirits and your spirits need to go back to where you first came [from] .... to become a human being again or whatever god plans you to be .... The song ... directs you step-by-step back. Even if an elder dies, every village or province or town that he lived in before, we take his spirit back ... until the original village that he was born .... That song is very long. It takes about three to five hours.*

Joe Bee Xiong
Eau Claire, December 15, 1992
Interviewer: James P. Leary

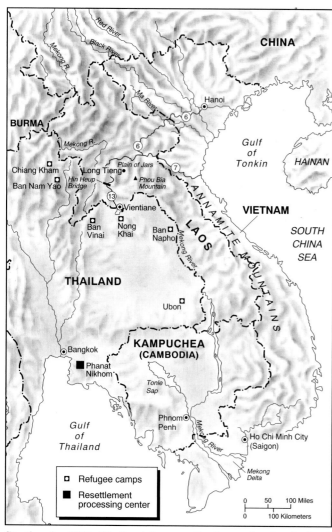

Starting in 1975, Thailand became the haven for hundreds of thousands of refugess from Vietnam, Laos and Cambodia. By December 1992, more than 213,000 Laotian lowlanders and nearly 150,000 Laotian highlanders (mostly Hmong) had sought asylum in Thailand. Map by Carto-Graphics.

The UNHCR coordinated relief efforts by member nations and voluntary agencies (volags). To cope with the shortage of space and material for housing, the UNHCR built long, tin-roofed row houses, hot boxes under a tropical sun. International relief agencies distributed needed food, clothing and medical supplies. Gradually conditions improved. Refugees grasped any opportunity to better their situation and overcome total dependency on relief. Silversmiths, needleworkers, and others found markets for their handcrafts. Families rented small plots for gardens. Children attended makeshift schools. At New Year, shamans swept away the past year's misfortunes and prepared for the festival of renewal.

Hot boxes under a tropical sun, tin-roofed row houses built by the United Nations stand alongside bamboo thatched houses at crowded Ban Vinai Refugee Camp, ca. 1983-85. Photographer: Jan Folsom.

Laying out a bedspread in dusty Ban Vinai Refugee Camp, ca. 1982-83. Photographer: Jan Folsom. Hmong women readily responded to outside efforts to market their needlework, sewing everything from pot-holders to Christmas tree skirts.

I lived in the camp for about eight years and would spend about 30 days to make four purses .... Back in our country, we only spent time sewing when we didn't have anything else to do, so we made paj ntaub *[needlework] for the New Year only. But at the camp in Thailand we didn't have anything to work on, so we spent more time working on* paj ntaub *and sent it all to my sisters, cousins, aunts, and nieces to sell [in the United States]. They sent the money back to us*

Bao Vang
Eau Claire, January 19, 1993
Interviewer: Tim Pfaff
Translator: Smidchei Xiong

Relief Efforts and "Picture Cloths"

World Relief, Save the Children, the Christian and Missionary Alliance (CAMA), and other volags mobilized resources to raise living standards and prepare refugees for probable resettlement. In 1976, CAMA set up a self-help program to market the striking needlework made by Hmong women. CAMA staff provided raw materials, advised on colors and styles likely to sell in foreign markets, and often designed new products. Jan Folsom, a textile designer hired by CAMA to develop and refine the project, recalled that Hmong women eagerly embraced the novel idea of selling their needlework, yet found it hard to fathom the use of products like toaster covers and crib liners. After several years, refugee-made bedspreads and Christmas tree skirts with appliqued Hmong designs began appearing in stores all over the world.

Designer Jan Folsom worked with refugee women to select patterns and color combinations that would appeal to an international clientele, Ban Vinai Refugee Camp, 1984. Jan Folsom.

Above: "Picture" or "story" cloth, made by Mai Xao Yang, Eau Claire, 1991. Hmong women experimented with subjects and colors. Some picture cloths illustrated folk tales, village life, or the exodus from Laos. Others, like this one, simply presented familiar animals and flowers. Below: Paj ntaub purse, made by Mai Bao Lee, ca. 1989. Elizabeth Perkins. Women sometimes added a thin layer of plastic onto their needlework in the refugee camps because of the dusty conditions. American consumers mistakenly viewed the plastic as an added decoration.

Picture cloths, or storycloths, which evolved in the camps, were an outgrowth of earlier educational efforts. Missionaries had collected Hmong folk tales in Laos in the 1960s to use in school primers. They taught Hmong men to draw characters to illustrate the books. Years later, faced with the unwelcome idleness of refugee camp life, men continued to draw, and Hmong women experimented with transferring the illustrations to cloth. They soon realized that, like other needlework, picture cloths could be marketed to foreigners. With time on their hands, Hmong artists created elaborate tapestries. Husbands and wives cooperated: men drew characters, women embroidered fabric. In the United States, picture cloths sold easily, often providing Americans with their first glimpses of Hmong culture and recent history. After some Hmong resettled in the United States, they began marketing needlework, providing an important source of income for relatives in the camps.[90]

Saying goodbye at Ban Vinai, many Hmong refugees wept at yet another scattering of their families, ca. 1985. Photographer: Jan Folsom.

Where Do We Go From Here?

I had a very difficult time to make decision ... to come to America .... Many, many ways make me not want to come .... I do not have any education in my entire life .... I do not know how to live without my mother, or my brothers and sisters .... My life in the future is real dark .... It took me two months .... We were out of money ... [My husband] Kay had to go out and work for ... the Thai farmer to cut trees - big trunk trees for very little pay. For a week ... he gone and when he comes home with his group he brought me ... a couple hundred baht [about $5]. And he hands me the money but he also showed me his hands. They all blisters from side to side. He make me tears. I say if we

I talked to my wife [Houa] that life in the camp is just only today. We don't know tomorrow, who going to die, because people die everyday. And maybe we will take a chance to go to America .... Finally, we made a decision .... Call our family together ... my uncle and a couple of the close family, we have a celebration .... On April 1st, we start our journey to Bangkok ... that morning my mother-in-law almost faint. She screamed and she almost died that morning .... We talk to my mother-in-law, "Please don't cry. When we get to America, we will make some way to get you out of here and to be united in America with our family."

Yong Kay Moua
Eau Claire, October 16, 1992
Interviewer: Tim Pfaff

don't go to a third country, and we continue to live like this ... "Is my husband going to be a slave?... Is it worth for me to delay?"

... Early morning came, I think it was as early as 6:00. We were ready on the bus line .... My mother was the one most painful who going to stay. She was afraid ... she and I will never see each other again. So our way of leaving —from Nong Khai to Bangkok, Thailand to come to Eau Claire [Wisconsin] —was almost like a funeral.

Houa Vue Moua
Eau Claire, May 10, 1993
Interviewer: Tim Pfaff

My brother and I decided that we wished to come to the United States because we don't really know how long we will be waiting in [Ban Vinai Camp] Thailand before our family can come .... We never thought that they couldn't come .... When you register, they ask you questions like "What did your parents do?... Were you in the Army?" We gave the United States personnel our family history .... If your [family members served] with the Army, what rank they have, they served in what area, in what battalion, company .... Then about one month later they came back and do another interview and if you pass that interview then you go to the third interview which is the one that you had to meet with [CIA case officer] Jerry [Daniels], who is the head of the group .... When I came, there was long lines because during that time the Hmong had just lost the war, the second war ... 1979-80.

Kao Xiong
Eau Claire, Oct. 26, 1992
Interviewer: Tim Pfaff

Few Hmong left Laos intending to move to the United States. Most believed only that they had to flee, and saw Thailand as a temporary safe haven until the political climate stabilized and they could return. As reality set in, refugees reluctantly accepted the idea of relocating. France, with its historic ties to the region, accepted a small percentage. The overwhelming majority —more than 100,000—chose the United States.

Former soldiers and USAID employees, at greatest risk due to their American associations, received priority. In May 1975, Congress passed the Indochina Migration and Refugee Assistance Act, exempting Indochinese refugees from the usual immigration restrictions. State Department and CIA employees who had previously worked in Laos with the Hmong interviewed those wishing to apply. From 1975-79, the United States accepted more than 20,000 Hmong. In 1980, President Carter exercised discretionary powers allocated under the Congressional Refugee Act and admitted 150,000 refugees from Southeast Asia.[91] In part, Carter was responding to widespread media attention to the plight of Cambodian and Laotian refugees. As a result, in 1980 more than 27,000 Laotian highlanders came to the United States. By 1993, the cumulative figure exceeded 110,000.

Photograph carried by Hmong veteran to prove that he had been an American ally. Former soldiers and their families received preference in resettlement due to perceived dangers of their repatriation to Laos. Timothy Castle.

A highly charged political issue, resettlement caused trauma for those leaving and those left behind. Families were split apart, and few could know when they might be reunited. In Laos, Hmong men had commonly taken more than one wife, especially during the war when they adopted wives and children of slain brothers. Resettlement forced them to choose. A common Hmong expression—To be with family is to be happy, to be without family is to be lost —foretold many tear-filled good-byes.[92]

Despite their experience working with Americans during the war, the first wave of Hmong refugees arrived in the United States in 1976 with little preparation for American life. Most spoke no English. Letters and cassette tapes to relatives back in the camps carried dispirited tales of economic hardships and social isolation. Those who dreamed of returning to Laos used such tales to exaggerate existing fears. For years, armed resistance groups used Thai refugee camps as bases for periodic raids across the border.

In 1980, U.S. policymakers anticipated that the second wave of refugees would arrive with far less education and experience than those already struggling in the United States. To "accelerate refugee self-sufficiency," the State Department responded by funding an Overseas Training Program. The program required all refugees (under age 55) to complete a 20-week preparatory course at Phanat Nikhom, Thailand, run by the consortium of Save the Children, the Experiment in International Living, and World Education. Instructors taught "survival English," community living skills, and work orientation. Refugees simulated a trip to the grocery store or a job interview. Younger students attended classes set up to mirror the American school system, complete with a cafeteria, volleyball team, and parent-teacher conferences.[93]

Clan leaders in Laos were not as powerful as when the Hmong migrated from Laos to Thailand .... [Stronger clan leadership] was necessary in the camps .... When the Hmong migrated from China to Laos, clan leaders had been important in leading people to the south. As the Hmong migrated from Laos to the United States, clan leaders were [again] the most important people because there were no longer naibans or tassengs to help resolve disputes and other family issues ....

Chia Koua Xiong
Eau Claire, August 25, 1994
Interviewer: Smidchei Xiong
Translator: Kao Xiong

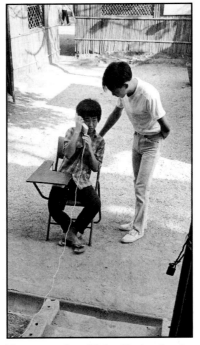

*Left: **Preparing for America**, Kia Lor (seated, center) attends an English as a Second Language class. Right: Her brother-in-law **Pao Lee learns how to answer a telephone**, Phanat Nikhom, Thailand, August 1987. Photographer: Neal Menschel, ©The Christian Science Monitor.*

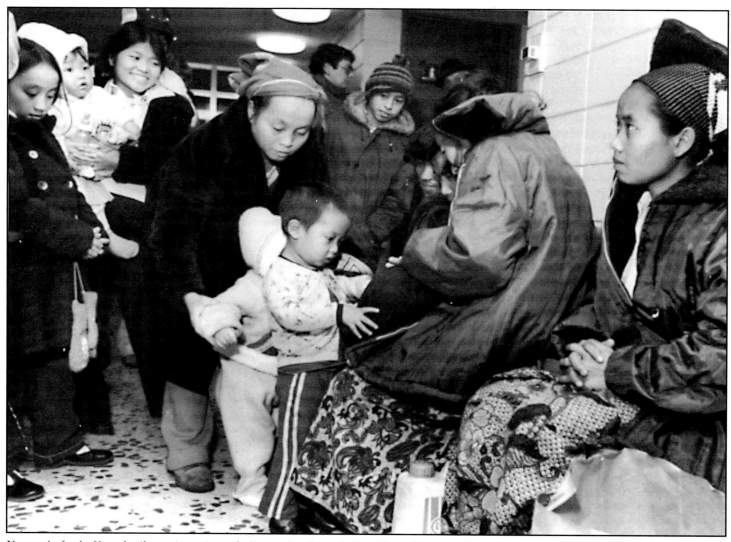

New arrivals, *the Vang family receives winter clothing at the airport in Eau Claire, Wisconsin, December 4, 1979. Photographer: John Lindrud,* Eau Claire Leader-Telegram. *Our Savior's Lutheran Church in Menomonie sponsored the family through Lutheran Immigration and Refugee Services.*

Chapter IV: Becoming Hmong Americans

It is difficult to overstate the culture shock experienced by Hmong resettling in the United States. Packing horrible memories of war and flight, they left behind squalid refugee camps to begin new lives in a highly industrialized, technologically driven consumer society. They faced significant linguistic, educational, economic, cultural and racial barriers which created confusing, embarrassing, and even frightening situations in their daily lives. Most had never lived in a house with plumbing or electricity and had little familiarity with common household appliances. Automobiles, telephones, televisions, and computers — icons of modern American life — had remained on the periphery of their experience. With a world view which valued, first and foremost, the welfare of the family and group, Hmong refugees attempted to cultivate the lands of the "rugged individual."

They came in waves beginning in the fall of 1975, cresting in the late 1970s and early 1980s, and slowing to a trickle in the 1990s. The migration's long time span required multiple services to assist refugees at various stages of the resettlement experience. In 1995, many Hmong Americans who have obtained training and employment are again self-sufficent. They often have children educated entirely in American schools, children who have little or no memories of Laos. At the same time, other Hmong adults have only recently made the journey to America. Many had spent years in Thai refugee camps, the only home their children had known prior to resettlement. They are just beginning the slow and difficult transition to American life, a journey affecting men and women, elders and children in strikingly different ways.

Settling In

Moua family arrives in Eau Claire, April 9, 1976. Above: At the airport. Below (front to back): Mary Boe, Houa Moua, husband Yong Kay Moua with Va Meng, Pastor Andy Boe, Kay's brothers Lo Pao and Dang Moua, Pastor Jack Olson. Lo Pao holds his nephew Va Meng. Sponsors from Trinity Lutheran Church helped the family get settled in a trailer in nearby Altoona. Trinity Lutheran Church Archives.

When we got to Eau Claire, it was April 9th [1976], about five in the evening .... a little dark, raining a little bit .... still very cold for us. We wondering, when we get out of the plane .... Everything ... looks different ... the people ... the buildings. When we get to a building, I think a whole group of people stand there and wave at us, and they tell us "We are your sponsors [Trinity Lutheran Church members] ...." They have some flowers, some fruit ... and all the warm clothes for us. We kind of think in our mind ... "Wow, these are the people who sponsored us ... and they are so friendly ...."

They brought us to Altoona, to the trailer court .... They already have some people there cooking .... They knew that we were very tired .... It is very tiring ... about 27 or 28 hours on the plane. You still feel that maybe the plane kind of going up and down .... My wife [Houa] was pregnant. She was very tired, very sick .... In the morning ... we look out the window, all the trailer houses were kind of quiet ... We wonder, "Why in this little town, or this little village, no people at all?..."

Life is just like you started very in the bottom ... They had to care for us, help us — how to do dishes, how to wash the clothes .... They show us like ... starting a new life, just like a baby. And we kind of wondering how life in America is going to be? Not just only days, but even a couple of months, we still wondering what we going to do and how we are going to get our life started again?

Yong Kay Moua
Eau Claire, October 16, 1992
Interviewer: Tim Pfaff

Individuals and voluntary agencies, such as the U.S. Catholic Conference, Lutheran Immigration and Refugee Services, and Church World Services, sponsored the first wave of Hmong refugees to the United States. Sponsors located housing, covered initial rent payments, arranged for appropriate food, clothing, housewares, and bedding, and oriented new arrivals to their host community.[94] The geographical dispersion of sponsoring groups accounted in part for a haphazard distribution of Hmong refugees across the country in cities such as Providence, Philadelphia, Chicago, St. Paul, Seattle, and Santa Ana.

The U.S. State Department encouraged placement of small numbers of refugees in many sites to lessen the economic impact on individual communities. Such policies heightened Hmong feelings of isolation. Many refugees relocated, shortly after their arrival, to join relatives in other cities. Over the next decade, "secondary migration" accounted for the growth of clusters of Hmong. The *Hmong Resettlement Study*, funded by the U.S. Office of Refugee Resettlement in 1985, reported a total of 30 states hosting 72 Hmong communities, the largest in Fresno and St. Paul. Most communities had fewer than a thousand Hmong. An extremely high birth-rate produced large families and a young population — 49 percent under age 15.[95]

Once refugees had established themselves in U.S. communities, they became the sponsors for relatives still in the camps. These later arrivals benefited from the experience and support of relatives but remained isolated from the non-Hmong community. The *Hmong Resettlement Study* noted that in 1982, 86 percent of the Hmong in Portland and 56 percent in Minneapolis-St. Paul had been sponsored by other Hmong families. In Minnesota and Wisconsin, active church sponsorship combined with secondary migration to produce what historian Alfred McCoy termed a "Hmong zone" extending from Minneapolis eastward to Lake Michigan. Twelve Wisconsin counties had Hmong communities of more than 1,000 by 1993, with the largest populations in Milwaukee, Wausau, Sheboygan, Appleton, Green Bay, La Crosse, Eau Claire and Oshkosh.

With a current Hmong population of about 2,300, Eau Claire reflects the challenges involved in resettlement, faced by both refugees and host communities. Area churches began sponsoring Hmong families in 1976. Trinity Lutheran Pastor Andy Boe drew the family names Moua, Thao, and Vang at a church conference seeking sponsors. Early arrivals came straight from Thailand assisted by Lutheran Social Services and Catholic Charities. By 1980 the local Hmong popula-

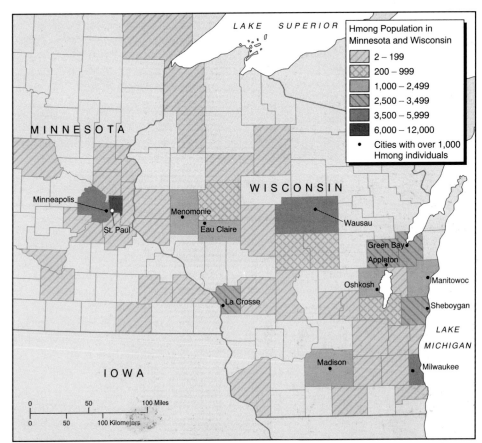

Hmong Resettlement Zone. *Clusters of Hmong have settled in communities from Minneapolis-St. Paul to southeastern Wisconsin. The 1990 census reported the largest populations in Minneapolis-St. Paul with 16,355 and Milwaukee with 5,347. Secondary migration accounts for steady growth. For example, the Wausau community has more than doubled since 1990 when the census reported 1,924. Map by Carto-Graphics.*

In 1987, I came to Eau Claire to visit my mother and her family .... My mother, who is so concerned about me ... said that she wanted me to go to school nearby and doesn't want me to go to school in Illinois because I am the only one in my family that is away .... Most of my family is here. My cousins/ relatives are here. The rest of my family came here in 1985. They actually came to Chicago but my older brother, Moua, said that he wanted to go here because most of my relatives are here. So he actually came to Chicago to pick them up and moved them to Eau Claire.

Kao Xiong
Eau Claire, Oct. 26, 1992
Interviewer: Tim Pfaff

Learning to live in America, *the Lee family has lunch in their Eau Claire apartment. August 1987. Photographer: Neal Menschel,* ©The Christian Science Monitor.

tion had increased to 300 as families traveled to Eau Claire from Philadelphia, Chicago, and other U.S. cities. In 1981, Jack O'Connell, Adult Basic Education Coordinator at the District I Technical College in Eau Claire, estimated that secondary migrants accounted for 80 percent of the local Hmong population.[96]

With limited financial resources, large families crammed into small, low-rent apartments in older neighborhoods. Housing became a chronic problem. The shortage of affordable housing prompted Hmong to rent apartments; yet families with many children ran into problems with the Housing Authority over legal limits on numbers of persons per room. Lacking knowledge of proper home maintenance, some Hmong mistreated their apartments and local landlords grew reluctant to have Hmong tenants.

Early arrivals — Yong Kay and Houa Vue Moua, Ger Vang, Yee Xiong, Kou Xiong, and Kou and Mai Xao Yang — received intensive assistance and language training from their sponsors. They then made up a core group of interpreters and community liaisons, assisting those who followed. Yong Kay Moua noted that at times he felt like "a ball being kicked from one to the other," as the needs of the growing community overwhelmed existing resources. In 1979, a Hmong Community Advisory Board consisting of Hmong leaders and representatives from local schools, city government, health care clinics, and social service agencies, was formed to address the needs of the growing refugee population. English as a Second Language (ESL) Programs were developed in Eau Claire area schools. Bilingual Hmong were hired as interpreters to assist law enforcement officials, health care professionals, and social service providers.

By 1982 the population had reached 600 and local leaders applied to the federal government to organize a Hmong Mutual Assistance Association (HMAA). The Eau Claire Parks and Recreation Department allocated office space in its building for Director Yee Xiong and a secretary. Their main task was to direct newcomers to available services. As the population grew, the organization grew along with it. With additional federal funding from the Federal Emergency Management Association (FEMA) and the state of Wisconsin, the HMAA relocated its offices and in 1987 added a case manager, job developer, and translation coordinator along with clerical staff. HMAA also operated a food pantry to provide rice and other necessities to newcomers until they began receiving food stamps.

Tou Lee receives a home visit from Lynn Santangelo, social worker for Lutheran Immigration and Refugee Service, Eau Claire, August 1987. Photographer: Neal Menschel, ©The Christian Science Monitor.

Yee Xiong served as the first director of the Eau Claire Area Hmong Mutual Assistance Association, October 27, 1984. Photographer: Dick Friedman, Eau Claire Leader-Telegram.

69

When I first came to Eau Claire,
I entered school in two weeks. I was
put into regular classes with Ameri-
can students. I didn't know any
English and I couldn't do any of the
school work. I only sat and listened
and watched them. When the teach-
ers were finished giving assign-
ments for the students, then they
came and helped me to write and
say a few words each day.

Chou Vue
Letter to the editor
Eau Claire Leader-Telegram
March 27, 1981

Kou Yang receives instruction from Judy Hamre *at the Chippewa Valley Technical College (CVTC), Eau Claire, November 22, 1980. Photographer: Jason Tetzloff,* Eau Claire Leader-Telegram. *At CVTC, Hmong adults studied English and Community Living Skills, along with classes ranging from welding to data entry.*

Survival English

Language represented the foremost barrier to successful resettlement. Without English, refugees could not advance in school, find jobs, or perform many routine tasks of daily life. A few Hmong in the first wave of resettlement arrived with a limited command of English through associations with American military and aid workers. Those who came after 1980 tended to come from more remote areas of Laos. They had little formal education and no English language training outside the Overseas Refugee Training Program.

Seventy percent of the Hmong could not read in their own language. French and American missionaries had developed the widely used Romanized Popular Alphabet (RPA) for the Hmong language in the early 1950s.[97] During the war, missionaries and USAID workers had helped to equip and run schools in Laos, but shifting battlelines made it difficult for many students to complete even a few years of classes. In the United States, many Hmong students faced the doubly difficult task of learning to read while also attempting to master a foreign language.

The Hmong language differs structurally from English in many ways. The Hmong do not add endings to indicate the tense of verbs or the plural of nouns. Other words in a sentence differentiate "jump" from "jumped" or "boy" from "boys." Hmong is also a tonal language. Each word contains one vowel sound whose tone or pitch contributes to the meaning of the word. In written form, final consonants are not pronounced but indicate different tones. For example, the words *pab* (to help), *paj* (flower), *pav* (to tie), *pa* (air), *pas* (stake), *pag* (part of a two-word name for a melon), and *pam* (blanket) acquire their specific meanings from the pitch of the speaker's voice.[98]

In Eau Claire, early arrivals received intensive tutoring from their sponsors. As the population grew, area schools and organizations provided ESL classes for all age groups. Schoolchildren learned quickly. They took a full schedule along with daily ESL classes. Teachers worked to "mainstream" them into age-appropriate grade levels as quickly as possible. ESL instructors used magazine cut-outs and toys so that students could see and touch what they were saying. Karen Alexander took walks with her Randall Elementary students, teaching them to name the things in their neighborhood. At Lincoln School, Alice Weikelt used a series of Hmong folk tales developed by linguist Charles Johnson, allowing students to learn English through familiar stories. After 1985, the school district hired bilingual Hmong teaching assistants.

Adults enrolled in ESL classes at the Chippewa Valley Technical College (CVTC) and the University of Wisconsin-Eau Claire (UWEC). UWEC professor Barbara Rolland started a program to train ESL instructors. Local non-profit organizations, such as VISTA, Literacy Volunteers of America, or the Retired Senior Volunteers Program (RSVP) tutored Hmong students in neighborhood classes. CVTC geared its program toward helping refugees achieve self-sufficiency quickly. Adults chose trades that they hoped would bring them high-wage factory jobs with little customer contact.

Above right: **ESL Reader,** *1981. Using familiar folk tales, linguist Charles Johnson from Macalester College, St. Paul, edited this series of beginning readers for ESL instruction. Below:* **Adults observe American agricultural practices** *on a visit to a farm outside Eau Claire. Western Dairyland RSVP.*

Making a Living

Most Hmong arrived knowing little about American life. Few spoke any English or brought skills that would enable them to gain meaningful employment. Initially, the federal government provided financial assistance for 36 months through the Refugee Cash Assistance program, after which, unable to support themselves, most refugees applied for existing state benefits. The federal government also provided funds for language and job training, and reimbursed states for their contributions to Aid to Families With Dependent Children (AFDC), Supplementary Security Insurance (SSI), Food Stamps, and Medicaid. Following the economic recession of 1981-82, the federal government reduced Refugee Cash Assistance from 36 to 18 months of coverage. The reduction, on the heels of some 43,000 new arrivals between 1979 and 1981, contributed to the secondary migration of refugees to states with more favorable eligibility requirements for financial assistance. By 1988, 85 percent of Hmong in America resided in California, Minnesota, and Wisconsin.[99]

The 1988 study, *Profiles of the Highland Lao Communities in the United States*, reported 63 percent of 105,253 Hmong in the United States on public assistance. Self-sufficiency of Hmong in particular communities ranged from 100 percent in Atlanta to zero in Eureka, California. The *Hmong Resettlement Study* (1985) found most Hmong adults eager to work but lacking language and job skills. The study also noted that eligibility requirements for state aid programs frequently presented significant work disincentives. A Hmong person could take a minimum-wage job to gain skills and experience, but would typically have to live on less money with no medical benefits for family members. Yet without that experience, self-supporting employment remained a distant possibility.[100]

Employment prospects also drove secondary migration. After word spread of modest successes made by a few Hmong farmers in the Fresno area in 1981, thousands flocked to California's Central Valley. The Hmong community soared to 8,000 in 1982, and to 12,000 the following year.[101] Unfortunately, Hmong generally were not able to farm successfully there. The combination of high land prices and an emphasis on high-tech agriculture produced a high unemployment rate. Hmong have had better success in industries requiring low-skilled manual labor, such as shrimp factories in Dallas-Ft. Worth, assembly and packaging plants in Providence, Rhode Island, or seasonal berry picking in Portland, Oregon.[102]

Sai Dang Xiong shows off the latest rice shipment at his Ameriental *Food Store, June 26, 1993. Photographer: Dan Reiland,* Eau Claire Leader-Telegram.

A few Hmong have had success starting small businesses, usually catering to other Hmong residents or building on traditional practices. In St. Paul, Hmong-owned "Oriental" grocery stores opened along University Avenue offering products not typically found in American food stores. Families purchased rice, for example, in 50-pound or 100-pound sacks. In Fresno, unable to farm on a large scale, Hmong turned instead to garden plots of 2-3 acres where they cultivated sugar peas, cherry tomatoes, chiles, and strawberries for sale locally. In Seattle and Missoula, Montana, craft cooperatives supplied *paj ntaub* and storycloths to specialty shops. In Wisconsin, needleworkers set up booths at festivals and craft shows.

Profiles of the Highland Lao listed only 14 percent of the Eau Claire area's 365 Hmong families as self-sufficient in 1988. Seventy families reported at least one member employed, but about 43 percent of those jobs were part-time. Men earned an average wage of $5.00; women, $4.50. Most families lived on an average income of $10,400. Only six students had graduated from college, although 61 were currently enrolled.[103]

Hmong gardeners sell summer produce at the Downtown Farmers' Market, Eau Claire, August 1994. Photographer: Jason Tetzloff.

Since 1988, Hmong dependency on public assistance in Eau Claire has steadily declined. The Wisconsin Policy Research Institute reported Hmong self-sufficiency at 30 percent in 1991.[104] HMAA Job Developer Jim Tout estimated that number at 40 percent in 1994. Fifty adults landed semi-skilled employment at Phoenix Steel, Minnesota Wire & Cable, Midwest Manufacturing, and, in nearby Baldwin, Donaldson Manufacturing. Twenty men and women worked in the Eau Claire school system, mostly as bilingual teaching assistants. A large percentage worked in Eau Claire city and county social service agencies, and at public and private health clinics.

Self-employment remained uncommon, mostly providing only supplementary income. Women sold needlework at area festivals and at the HMAA craft store. Families rented garden plots and sold produce at the Downtown Farmer's Market. Since 1992, the City of Eau Claire has sponsored an internship program which offers incentives for area businesses to provide job experience for Hmong adults. Tout predicted that Hmong self-sufficiency might rise to 70 percent over the next five years as more Hmong graduates enter the workforce.

My people could not read English, couldn't follow instructions on pesticide packages. Many get sick from the spray. We don't understand how to irrigate fields. In Laos, farmers just wait for rain. We don't understand marketing - one year farmers get high price for snow peas, next year almost nothing .... We thought ... if we farm, maybe we can be independent people again. But unfortunately, when we arrive in Central Valley [of California] we learn that you must have something else ... money.

Lang Lee, Director
United Lao Agricultural Assoc.
Fresno, August 1986
Interviewer: Frank Viviano
(Takaki, 464)

Hmong leaders in the United States operate on multiple levels, deriving their authority from previous status as military or civilian officials, clan membership, and knowledge of American systems. General Vang Pao was largely responsible for the Hmong community that resettled in Missoula. In 1977 he helped found Lao Family Community, Inc., a non-profit mutual assistance association for refugees in Santa Ana, which quickly became a national organization with many local affiliates. Vang Pao has remained a powerful although controversial figure.

Since 1981, Vang Pao has actively sought support and financial contributions from Hmong Americans to pursue armed resistance in Laos under the banner of the United Lao National Liberation Front.

Left to right: **Leaders Ge Moua, Vang Pao,** *and* **Yang Dao** *attend a New Year's celebration in Chicago, October 1980. Kao Xiong. Yang Dao has been a leading advocate for youth education in the United States. Col. Moua is a close associate of General Vang Pao.*

Commonly known as *Neo Hom*, the organization funded resistance fighters who attacked Laotian villages from their bases in Thai refugee camps. Raids against Hmong who have returned to Laos discouraged those still in the camps from repatriating. Hmong American families have been asked to pay $100 down and $10 per month to support the group's activities. In a 1984 letter to his supporters, Vang Pao noted that only those who contributed regularly would be considered permanent members of *Neo Hom* and, after "liberation," receive priority for positions in a new government.[105]

Critics contend that the resistance lacks widespread support in Laos. They charge that *Neo Hom* has failed to keep adequate financial records and question whether money contributed by Hmong Americans has actually reached the resistance. From 1981-89, regular contributors to *Neo Hom* declined from 80 percent of the U.S. Hmong to less than half. Opponents argue that financial donations have further impoverished refugee families already heavily dependent on public assistance.[106]

The explosive issue has created deep fissures within Hmong American communities, at times causing dissension within clans. Such divisions are worth noting because clan membership remains a central aspect of Hmong society. Clan allegiances helped Hmong maintain cultural cohesion during migrations from China to Laos, and Laos to Thailand. In the United States, clan leaders have found that their influence has transcended traditional marriage mediation to include a variety of issues, owing largely to the absence of elected Hmong political leaders. Clans offer security and mutual support to individuals and families attempting to regroup and rebuild in a strange land. Relatives followed leaders Wang Sher Xiong, Pa Cha Xiong, Nao Tou Xiong, Nhia Blia Xiong, and Chia Koua Xiong to Eau Claire, making Xiong the dominant clan in the area. In Des Moines, leader Lao Thai Vang's arrival prompted other Vang families to join him.[107]

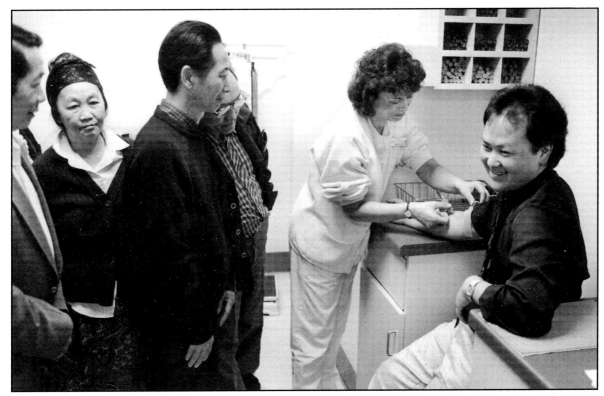

Smidchei Xiong submits to a blood test to sooth elders' fears about American medical procedures, Luther Hospital, May 26, 1990. Photographer: Dick Friedman, Eau Claire Leader-Telegram. Hmong culture in Laos observed strong taboos against surgery, believing that the act of cutting open the body would release the soul.

Younger men and, increasingly, women fluent in English and better able to cope with American systems, represent another source of leadership. They have acted as interpreters and liaisons between the Hmong and non-Hmong communities. Older clan leaders, who generally hold the power to mobilize the community, have relied on them to find "a path through the American woods."[108] In 1980, they began staffing Mutual Assistance Associations (MAAs), self-help organizations funded by the U.S. Office of Refugee Resettlement. MAAs identified sponsors, located housing, supplied food and household furnishings, and provided English language training, and translation and orientation services. As an ongoing function, MAAs have offered job training and placement, and generally have served as advocate and liaison for Hmong families attempting to negotiate American society. Over time, MAAs have also evolved into community centers, hosting New Year's celebrations, soccer tournaments, or the occasional pot-luck dinner.

... In this country, I think we look for people that can help us to move our life here in a different direction ... helping us with the job, with the services and with, what you call, transition into the new society .... The other leader that we look to in the community is the clan leader, that they helping ... with family conflicts, with the parent and children conflict. [For] this kind of leader we still look up to the older people ... kind of helping the family to stay together. That is why I said we have many leaders here .... If we talk about the leader that will lead us into education, job or communication, that will be a different one ... [than] the leader who help to put the community together, the family together ....

Yong Kay Moua
Eau Claire, November 16, 1992
Interviewer: Tim Pfaff

Cultural Confrontation and Confusion

The ability of Hmong refugees to adapt in the United States has varied according to such factors as age, gender, education, and the attitudes of host community residents. Many Americans have generously welcomed them by serving as sponsors, tutors, or mentors and donating clothing and household items. Others have not greeted refugees so graciously. Arriving after America's painful and divisive experience in Vietnam, many Hmong were spurned by angry Americans who mistakenly viewed them as Vietnamese. Some refugees have been spat upon on the streets or labeled "dog eaters." Many switched to unlisted telephone numbers after repeated hostile phone calls.[109]

In some cases, attitudes about the Hmong have failed to change with circumstances. For example, Hmong refugees who first rented apartments in Eau Claire in the late 1970s had little knowledge of American home maintenance practices and did damage some apartments. However, refugee educational services since then have greatly improved. In 1989, the Eau Claire Housing Authority produced a series of videos on American households to use as an orientation tool for refugees. Despite improvements in refugee education, Hmong continued to experience discrimination and, in some cases, abuse by local landlords who either refused to rent to them or took advantage of their naiveté by failing to provide basic services.[110]

Sometimes they [landlords] just hang up when they hear my voice is Hmong. I think they don't like Hmong people to live in their house .... Sometimes they say "You are Hmong and have too many people" even if I don't tell them how many children I have. Then they tell me I can't call them back .... I feel like this is not my country.

Kao Xiong
March 21, 1993
Eau Claire Leader-Telegram

Yong Kay Moua addresses a crowd gathered to discuss reports of harrassment, intimidation, and vandalism against Hmong people in Eau Claire, June 15, 1982. Photographer: John Lindrud, Eau Claire Leader-Telegram.

In other instances, tension over Hmong resettlement has less to do with racial discrimination than with limited resources. Large, rapid influxes of immigrants create problems for host communities which defy easy remedy. Wausau (population 37,500) is one of several small cities in Wisconsin that have attracted a large number of Hmong secondary migrants because of the relatively liberal AFDC eligibility requirements, high quality schools, and strong emphasis on technical education. In Wausau, Hmong clustered in poorer neighborhoods where housing was less expensive. As a result, their children were concentrated at just a few schools.

High Hmong birth rates ballooned elementary school enrollment. The Wausau School District's property-tax rate rose 10.48 percent in 1992, three times higher than for adjoining districts with few immigrants.[111]

The crux of the matter, however, was not simply taxes. Non-Hmong parents living in neighborhoods with high numbers of Hmong residents grew concerned that their children's education was being compromised. Hmong parents believed that if their children attended classes where they were the majority, they would not be adequately exposed to American culture and would fail to learn what they needed to know to succeed. The school board responded with a busing plan to distribute Hmong and non-Hmong students evenly throughout the district. Residents heatedly debated the plan for two years. The school board implemented it in September 1993. In December, those board members who had voted in favor of busing were removed from office in a recall election. The resulting polarization of the community persisted.[112]

Hmong students make up 62 percent of the enrollment at Lincoln Elementary School, Wausau, Wisconsin, April 1994. Photographer: ©Leonard Freed, ©MAGNUM.

Within Hmong American communities, members have varying resettlement experiences. Older people encounter the greatest difficulty making the adjustment. In fact, the Overseas Refugee Training Program did not even require those over 55 to participate. Older people feel most keenly the loss of their homeland and loved ones. They remain attached to traditional values and practices which are sometimes viewed by Americans as inappropriate or by younger Hmong people as irrelevant. Older people complain that they are unable to discipline their children under American law and that, coupled with the lack of respect afforded elders, increasingly propels teens into gang violence. Left at home as baby-sitters, they endure the frustration and humiliation of having grandchildren interpret for them.

Hmong men and women have also had conflicting adjustment experiences. Traditional gender roles began to erode during the war when Hmong women engaged in trade to help feed their families. As refugees in Thai camps, wives often coped better than husbands. They were able to continue many of their usual activities, such as keeping house and child-rearing, while their needlework earned indispensable income which husbands found difficult to match. In the United States, American views about the equality of the sexes and the need for multiple family incomes accelerated this transition, although not without resistance. Hmong men continue to occupy most leadership roles in the community, and husbands take priority over

I feel bad because I have been in this country for three years and no one has taught me a word in English. My vision is getting worse .... I must put my glasses on when I want to read .... I feel bad because I don't know how to drive .... how to communicate with any Americans .... When I think about it I cry by myself. I keep all the sadness in my heart. I see some Hmong people know how to read, know how to drive .... When Americans knock on the door, they know how to welcome them. When Americans ask the address, they know what to say. It seems like they know everything .... If I was still young and came to this country with the knowledge I have, I would have learned to speak English. In Laos I didn't have problems with anyone .... I was a good person.

Chia Koua Xiong
Eau Claire, November 5, 1992
Interviewer: Smidchei Xiong
Translator: Kao Xiong

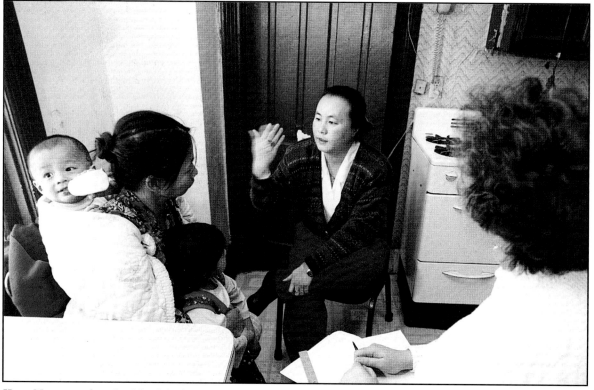

Houa Moua translates health advice *from registered nurse Monica Pittman to Chou Xiong, March 16, 1994. Photographer: Dan Reiland*, Eau Claire Leader-Telegram. *Moua works as a translator for the Eau Claire City/County Health Department.*

wives in English classes, job training, and employment. However, needleworkers continue to earn income. Hmong women increasingly work in Hmong organizations, as bilingual teaching assistants in schools, and as interpreters for public agencies. Future generations of Hmong women, having been educated in American schools, will likely pursue career goals comparable to those of their non-Hmong classmates.

Young people find themselves torn between the desire of elders to preserve culture and the demands of American society to assimilate. Those who came to the United States as infants or were born in this country have a hard time embracing Hmong culture. They play with the same toys and watch the same television shows as their non-Hmong schoolmates. They make comparisons between themselves and their peers. In school they read about George Washington and Abraham Lincoln, and find role models in Michael Jordan or Hillary Rodham Clinton. As teens, they are more interested in learning the guitar than the *qeej*.

Above: **Brothers and cousins Yeng, Nou, Neng, Cher, Seng, and Sa Xiong** *formed the band* XyoojVij Zeej *(Surrounding People) mixing a contemporary Laotian sound with American rock, May 1994. Right: Older brother* **Joe Bee Xiong demonstrates the qeej** *outside his home in Eau Claire, May 12, 1994. Photographer: David Joles, Eau Claire Leader-Telegram. Xiong, a master* qeej *player, also teaches Hmong traditional music to young people.*

The process of change has frequently been painful. Teenage girls may risk ostracism when they put off marriage until after graduation. Hmong weddings involving "bride captures" have brought police inquiries and unwanted headlines. In Laos, it was considered acceptable for a man to abduct his intended bride, removing her to the home of his parents. Within 24 hours after the "capture," he was required to send representatives back to the bride's parents to seek their approval and mediate the marriage agreement which would involve a "bride price" paid in silver bars. In some cases, the bride and groom had already secretly agreed to marry. The formality of the capture and the bride's feigned unwillingness demonstrated the woman's respect for her parents and the man's commitment to the marriage. In other cases, the bride's resistance was sincere, yet she had little choice.

We play traditional qeej *[songs] here, but we realize that it is very hard for us to reserve a funeral [home] for three to four days. If two Hmong people died at the same time, then we want one funeral to end before the other opens .... We do not have enough help in the community to perform the traditional funeral .... Back in Laos, we call the coffin the horse, but in the United States ... we call the coffin the airplane because when we came we flew on an airplane. So we tell the spirits that you need to take the airplane back. We still guide the dead person way back past China, crossing freezing death terrain, crossing the plain of caterpillars that sting people.*

Joe Bee Xiong
Eau Claire, December 15, 1992
Interviewer: James P. Leary

When I came to this country I had made my mind that I don't want to force my children to marry. I thought [about] myself ... my parents and my brother force me to marry, and I not that happy .... So I told my kids, all my girls, that I will change, I don't want to keep the old thing like that because, myself, I [was] not happy. And if you find somebody you like, you want to marry, fine. But if somebody take you away or somebody come to the house ... you know for the tradition, if people come to the house, it's very important to the parent of the clan, they gotta give you away. So I will not do that anymore.

Mai Xao Yang
Madison (WI), August 22, 1994
Interviewer: Tim Pfaff

Kou Yang (back) and Mai Xao Yang (right) gathered children *and friends to celebrate their daughter Pa Foua's high school graduation, Eau Claire, June 1986. A straight-A student at North High School, Pa Foua (second from left) went on to college and medical school. Photographer: Jan Folsom.*

In Laos ... Hmong never allowed their daughter to have free choice. ... They want the boyfriend to say, "I want to marry this daughter" ... But if the girl likes the guy, then she won't say anything about it. And so if this guy came ... said "I want to marry you," she said, "Sure, you can marry me, but to do that you got to hold my hand and tell my parents how you really want me. No matter [if] I'm screaming and yelling or whatever .... Sometimes you can give like a couple hundred dollars or $1,000 to a girl and say, "Do you want to promise you will marry me? Will you keep my money?" And the parents have to be able to find ... that promissory item, and be able to prove she is not kidnapped, [but] is actually wanting to marry him and just holding back .... sometimes when we talk about kidnapping, it's really a big, big, big argument and discussion in the Hmong community, whether a case is kidnapping or it is not ....

Kao Xiong
Eau Claire, Oct. 26, 1992
Interviewer: Tim Pfaff

Americans have labeled the practice kidnapping whether or not the Hmong woman agreed to the marriage. In some cases, Hmong men have been arrested. In others, women have been criticized for seeking the protection of American law. The practice has stirred deep feelings within the Hmong community and illustrates the vast gulf separating the two cultures.

Dilemmas Unresolved

For Hmong families in the 1990s, the war, refugee status, and adjustment to American life are pressing issues that continue to invade their daily lives. Relocation depression is widespread, particularly among older people unable to cope with their new surroundings. Like returning American Vietnam War veterans, elders still carry powerful memories of bombs and firefights. Many refugees suffer from frequent nightmares as well as "survivor guilt," wondering why they lived through the ordeal that took so many relatives and friends. Some have died in their sleep, suddenly and mysteriously. Physicians have been unable to explain the cause of "Hmong sudden-death syndrome," an affliction that has taken the lives of more than 100 former soldiers between the ages 30-50. Family members speculate that the cause is intense grief.[113]

Disputes over whether to support ongoing armed resistance in Laos continue to divide Hmong American communities. In recent years, improved relations between Thai and Laotian governments have made Thai officials less tolerant of Hmong resistance activities launched from refugee camps. In June 1991, representatives from the Thai and Laotian governments, meeting with UNHCR, agreed upon a three-phased repatriation plan to close the camps. Remaining Hmong refugees, estimated at 44,000, had to choose between

Protesting the closing of Thai refugee camps and repatriation of Hmong to Laos, demonstrators march outside the State Capitol in St. Paul, Minnesota, February 3, 1990. Photographer: Jon Ahlberg.

81

*Above: Relatives remaining in Northern Laos, 1990. Khoua Yang. Hmong refugees have begun returning to Laos, some to live, others only to visit. Below: **Ker Yang and her cousin** on their way to New Year in Eau Claire, ca. 1988. Karen Alexander. In Wisconsin, the celebration is in October to avoid winter driving conditions.*

returning to Laos or resettling in a third country. Officials hoped that by the end of 1994 all camps would be closed.

The plan fell behind schedule for numerous reasons. Many Hmong were reluctant to go back to Laos out of genuine fear for their safety there. In March 1992, Hmong Americans staged demonstrations in several U.S. cities protesting human rights violations against Hmong in Laos and calling for an end to what they termed "forced repatriation." Undocumented stories of Pathet Lao reprisals against the Hmong remain widespread. Many refugees who would volunteer for repatriation are intimidated by resistance fighters who oppose the closing of the camps as a significant hindrance to their activities.[114]

> There are lots of people in Na Pho and Chian Kham who are willing to go back [to Laos] but they are not willing to say so publicly. If they do, several things happen: MOI [Thai Ministry of Interior] comes and says they must sign a paper that they could go back within a few days. The other thing is they get pressure from people in the camps. I had a firebomb thrown at my house for talking about voluntary repatriation in Ban Vinai. I felt it was no longer safe to stay there.
>
> Two groups want the refugees to stay in Thailand. One is the resistance, and they are getting money from overseas [United States].... The other is local Thai officials who are also making money off the camps.
>
> Vue May
> Ban Vinai camp leader, 1980-91
> Interview, August 1992
> (Robinson, 6)

The Thai government has, however, remained committed to the process. In July 1992, the government arrested and deported seven Hmong dissidents holding U.S. passports for alleged guerrilla activities in Laos. In October, Vang Fung (brother to Vang Pao) and Moua Lee Julan were also arrested and deported. Both were accused of planning a raid into Sayaboury Province timed to coincide with a goodwill visit of the daughter of Thailand's King Bhumidol Adulyadej.[115]

Despite UNHCR claims that it is safe for Hmong refugees to return to Laos, most have chosen resettlement to the United States. From January 1991 to June 1994, the U.S. accepted nearly 25,000 Hmong refugees. Another 2,736 await resettlement at Phanat Nikhom processing center. Ban Vinai closed at the end of 1992. Chiang Kham closed the following year. As of August 1994, some 7,938 Hmong refugees remained at Na Pho camp, scheduled for closure in 1995.

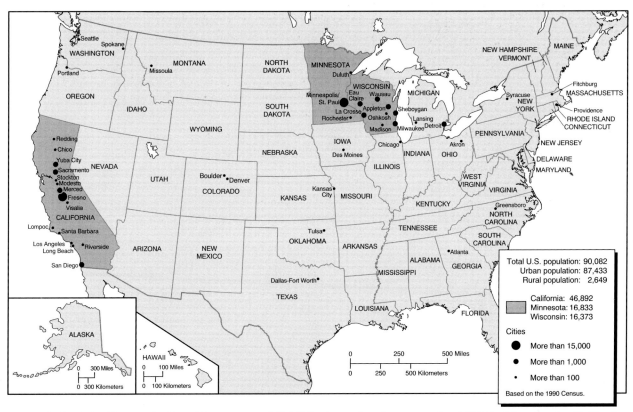

Hmong in the United States. *The United States accepted 225,675 refugees from Laos, more than 110,000 of them Laotian highlanders, from FY 1975 to FY 1993. Despite State Department efforts to spread refugees around the country, Hmong have tended to relocate to join families and clan relatives. Map by Carto-Graphics.*

I don't know any Hmong that doesn't have reminders of his own country. They have brothers, sisters, or parents there. But our future is in the United States, and we plan for a future in the United States.

Sy Moua
November 22, 1980
Eau Claire Leader-Telegram

Yong Kay Moua welcomes his mother, Nao Yang, *at the Eau Claire airport, May 18, 1993. Photographer: John Lindrud,* Eau Claire Leader-Telegram.

Epilogue

On March 18, 1993, the front page of the *Eau Claire Leader-Telegram* spoke volumes about the Hmong experience. Yong Kay Moua embraced his mother, Nao Yang, after nearly 20 years of separation. Moua, one of the first Hmong refugees to resettle in Eau Claire, had been a leader in the community, helping to establish the Hmong Mutual Assistance Association and the job internship program with the City of Eau Claire. Nao Yang, who had been living in Ban Vinai Refugee Camp for more than five years, was just beginning the difficult transition to American life.

Notes

Chapter I - Across the Mountaintops of Laos

1 Herold J. Wiens, *China's March Toward The Tropics* (Hamden, Connecticut: The Shoe String Press, 1954), 36, 68; Keith Quincy, *Hmong: History of a People* (Cheney, Washington: Eastern Washington University Press, 1988), 12-32; Dao Yang, Ph.D., *Hmong at the Turning Point* (Minneapolis: WorldBridge Associates, Ltd., 1993), xvi.

2 Wiens, 202; Alfred W. McCoy, Cathleen B. Read, and Leonard P. Adams II, *The Politics of Heroin in Southeast Asia* (New York: Harper & Row, 1972), 79.

3 McCoy, *The Politics of Heroin*, 79-80; Wiens, 235.

4 Wiens, 91, 190-200; Barbara J. Rolland and Houa Vue Moua, *Trail Through the Mists* (Eau Claire, Wisconsin: By the authors, 1994), 42.

5 McCoy, *The Politics of Heroin*, 80; Yang, 12, 25; Gary Y. Lee, "Minority Policies and the Hmong," in *Contemporary Laos: Studies in the Politics and Society of the Lao People's Democratic Republic*, ed. Martin Stuart-Fox (St. Lucia: University of Queensland Press, 1982), 199.

6 G. Linwood Barney, "The Hmong of Northern Laos." M.A. thesis, University of Minnesota, 1957, in *Indochinese Refugee Education Guides: Glimpses of Hmong History and Culture* (Washington, D.C.: Center for Applied Linguistics, November 1980), 23.

7 Charles Johnson and Se Yang, eds. *Myths, Legends and Folk Tales from the Hmong of Laos* (St. Paul: Macalester College, 1985, reprint 1992), 155; Yang, 23-25.

8 Yang, 17; Barney, 29-30.

9 Johnson, 264-65; W.E. Garrett, "The Hmong of Laos: No Place to Run," *National Geographic* 145 (January 1974): 94.

10 Yang, 50-53.

11 Johnson, 292.

12 Susan Lindbergh Miller, Bounthavy Kiatoukaysy, and Tou Yang, eds., *Hmong Voices in Montana* (Missoula, Montana: Missoula Museum of the Arts Foundation, 1993), 37.

13 Yang, 77.

14 Sally Peterson, "From the Heart and the Mind: Creating *Paj Ntaub* in the Context of Community," (Ph.D. diss., University of Pennsylvania, 1990), 109-19; Joanne Cubbs, "Hmong Art: Tradition and Change," in *Hmong Art: Tradition and Change* (Sheboygan, Wisconsin: John Michael Kohler Arts Center, 1986), 24.

15 Yang, 61; Peterson, 79.

16 Cubbs, in *Hmong Art*, 23-24.

17 Barney, 37-42.

18 Johnson, 64-67.

19 Alfred W. McCoy, "French Colonialism in Laos, 1893-1945," in *Laos: War and Revolution*, eds. Nina S. Adams and Alfred W. McCoy (New York: Harper & Row, 1970), 67-75.

20 Geoffrey C. Gunn, *Political Struggles in Laos, 1930-54: Vietnamese Communist Power and the Struggle for National Independence* (Bangkok: Editions Duang Kamol, 1988), 28-29; McCoy, in *Laos: War and Revolution*, 75-76.

21 McCoy, in *Laos: War and Revolution*, 77-78; Gunn, 30; Yang, 26-29.

22 McCoy, *The Politics of Heroin*, 72-76; Arthur J. Dommen, *Conflict in Laos: The Politics of Neutralization* (New York: Praeger, 1971), 16-17.

23 McCoy, *The Politics of Heroin*, 76-77.

24 Yang, 76-80; Catherine Lamour and Michel R. Lamberti, *The International Connection: Opium from Growers to Pushers* (New York: Pantheon Books, 1974), 116; Garrett, 103.

25 Yang, 37-38; McCoy, in *Laos: War and Revolution*, 81, 91-92.

26 McCoy, *The Politics of Heroin*, 82-84.

27 Gunn, 225-27; Jane Hamilton-Merritt, *Tragic Mountains: The Hmong, the Americans, and the Secret Wars for Laos, 1942-1992* (Indianapolis: Indiana University Press, 1993), 19-36.

28 Gunn, 227.

29 McCoy, *The Politics of Heroin*, 78-85.

Chapter II - The Secret War

30 Marvin E. Gettleman, Jane Franklin, Marilyn Young, and H. Bruce Franklin, eds., *Vietnam and America: A Documented History* (New York: Grove Press, Inc., 1985), 25-66.

31 Timothy Castle, *At War in the Shadow of Vietnam: U.S. Military Aid to the Royal Lao Government, 1955-75* (New York: Columbia University Press, 1992), 8.

32 McCoy, in *Laos: War and Revolution*, 92-95.

33 Arnold R. Isaacs, Gordon Hardy, and MacAlister Brown, eds., *Pawns of War: Cambodia and Laos* (Boston: Boston Publishing Co., 1987), 24.

34 Nina S. Adams, "Patrons, Clients and Revolutionaries: The Lao Search for Independence, 1945-1954," in *Laos: War and Revolution*, eds. Nina S. Adams and Alfred W. McCoy (New York: Harper & Row, 1970), 100-20.

35 Dommen, 87-93.

36 Gary D. Wekkin, "The Rewards of Revolution: Pathet Lao Policy towards the Hill Tribes Since 1975," in *Contemporary Laos: Studies in the Politics and Society of the Lao People's Democratic Republic*, ed. Martin Stuart-Fox (St. Lucia: University of Queensland Press, 1982), 186; McCoy, *The Politics of Heroin*, 92-109.

37 Castle, 10; McCoy, *The Politics of Heroin*, 102, Interview with Gen. Edward G. Landsdale, Alexandria, Virginia, June 17, 1971, 264-265.

38 Isaacs, 30.

39 Castle, 11.

40 Len E. Ackland, "No Place for Neutralism: The Eisenhower Administration and Laos," in *Laos: War and Revolution*, eds. Nina S. Adams and Alfred W. McCoy (New York: Harper & Row, 1970), 141.

41 Castle, 15.

42 Ackland, in *Laos: War and Revolution*, 143; Bernard B. Fall, *Anatomy of a Crisis: The Laotian Crisis of 1960-61* (New York: Doubleday, 1969), 171.

43 Fall, 85-86; Dommen, 101.

44 Fall, 86.

45 Lee, in *Contemporary Laos*, 202.

46 Fall, 94-97; Dommen, 99-101.

47 Fall, 108.

48 Castle, 19; Dommen, 133.

49 Dommen, 114.

50 Dommen, 144-46; Peter S. Usowski, "Intelligence Estimates and U.S. Policy Toward Laos, 1960-63," *Intelligence and National Security*, 6, 2 (1991): 370.

51 Castle, 20-27.

52 Usowski, 374.

53 Castle, 29.

54 Castle, 29-32.

55 Castle, 38; Office of Refugee Resettlement, *Hmong Resettlement Study, Volume I, Final Report* (Washington, D.C.: U.S. Department of Health and Human Services, Social Security Administration, April 1985), 18-19.

56 Hamilton-Merritt, 53; McCoy, *The Politics of Heroin*, 268-69.

57 Hamilton-Merritt, 97-98.

58 Interview with Touby Lyfoung, Vientiane, Laos, September 1, 1971, in McCoy, *The Politics of Heroin*, 268.

59 Lee, in *Contemporary Laos*, 202; Hamilton-Merritt, 90.

60 Don Schanche, *Mister Pop* (New York: David McKay, 1970), 64-65, 73; Castle, 40; McCoy, *The Politics of Heroin*, 271-74.

61 Schanche, 79-116; Castle, 59-60.

62 Isaacs, 71-72.

63 Castle, 99.

64 Grant Evans, *The Yellow Rainmakers: Are Chemical Weapons Being Used in Southeast Asia?* (London: Verso, 1983), 16; Garrett, 83, 89.

65 Castle, 80-82.

66 Christopher Robbins, *Air America* (New York: G.P. Putnam's Sons, 1979), 104-05.

67 Castle, 82-83.

68 Castle, 94-97.

69 Castle, 96; Schanche, 298-302.

70 Schanche, 302; Castle, 105-07.

71 Robert Shaplen, *Time Out of Hand* (New York: Harper & Row, 1970), 352, in McCoy, *The Politics of Heroin*, 281.

72 Castle, 113.

73 Castle, 116.

Chapter III - Exodus to Thailand

74 Yang, 142; Castle, 115-21.

75 Lee, in *Contemporary Laos*, 203; Yang, 146-51.

76 Lee, in *Contemporary Laos*, 205; Yang, 155-56; Castle 125.

77 Bernard J. Van-es-Beeck, "Refugees from Laos, 1975-1979," in *Laos: Studies in the Politics and Society of the Lao People's Democratic Republic*, ed. Martin Stuart-Fox (St. Lucia: University of Queensland Press, 1982), 325; Hamilton-Merritt, 342-48.

78 Yang, 156.

79 Evans, 23-24; Lee, in *Contemporary Laos*, 206.

80 Yang, 13; Evans, 132.

81 Lee, in *Contemporary Laos*, 207-09.

82 Lee, in *Contemporary Laos*, 206-07; Quincy, 193.

83 Evans, 25, 28-30; Lee, in *Contemporary Laos*, 213.

84 Evans, 31-32; Hamilton-Merritt, 381-82; William A. Smalley, Chia Koua Vang, and Gnia Yee Yang, *Mother of Writing: The Origin and Development of a Hmong Messianic Script* (Chicago: University of Chicago Press, 1990), 26-39.

85 Evans, 33.

86 *Hmong Resettlement Study*, 25-26; Mace Goldfarb, M.D., *Fighters, Refugees, Immigrants: A Story of the Hmong* (Minneapolis: Carolrhoda Books, Inc., 1982), 14; Lynnellyn Long, *Ban Vinai: The Refugee Camp* (New York: Columbia University Press, 1993), 58; Robert Shaplen, "A Reporter at Large: Survivors," *New Yorker* 5 September, 1977: 33-36.

87 *Hmong Resettlement Study*, 27.

88 Goldfarb, 28.

89 Goldfarb, 12, 23-31.

90 *Hmong Resettlement Study*, 27.

91 Long, 36; Tricia Knoll, *Becoming Americans: Asian Sojourners, Immigrants, and Refugees in the Western United States* (Portland, Oregon: Coast to Coast Books, 1982), 141.

92 Goldfarb, 14.

93 *Passage: A Journal of Refugee Education* 2 (Spring 1986): inside cover.

Chapter IV - Becoming Hmong Americans

94 Knoll, 148.

95 Henry T. Trueba, Lila Jacobs, and Elizabeth Kirton, *Cultural Conflict and Adaptation: The Case of the Hmong Children in American Society* (New York: The Falmer Press, 1990), 39; *Hmong Resettlement Study*, 37-40.

96 October 20, 1981 Report, Papers of Jack O'Connell, Area Research Center, University of Wisconsin-Eau Claire.

97 Ronald Takaki, *Strangers from a Different Shore: A History of Asian Americans* (Boston: Little, Brown and Company, 1989), 463; Smalley, 151-54.

98 Knoll, 158; Amy Catlin, "The Hmong and Their Music ... A Critique of Pure Speech," in *Hmong Art: Tradition and Change* (Sheboygan, Wisconsin: John Michael Kohler Arts Center, 1986), 13.

99 Simon M. Fass, *The Hmong in Wisconsin: On the Road to Self-Sufficiency* (Milwaukee: The Wisconsin Policy Research Institute Report, April 1991), 4, 14-15; Doua Yang and David North, *Profiles of the Highland Lao* (Washington, D.C.: Office of Refugee Resettlement, U.S. Department of Health and Human Services, November 1988), 9.

100 *Hmong Resettlement Study*, 97.

101 David M. Abramson, "The Hmong: A Mountain Tribe Regroups in the Valley," *California Living Magazine* 29 January 1984, 10.

102 *Hmong Resettlement Study*, Appendix 1.

103 Yang, *Profiles of the Highland Lao*, 93.

104 Fass, 19.

105 Ruth Hammond, "The Great Refugee Shakedown: The Hmong Are Paying to Free Laos - But What's Happening to the Money?" *The Washington Post* 16 April 1989, B1.

106 Hammond, B4; Ruth Hammond, "Rumors of War." *Twin Cities Reader* 25-31 October 1989, 8-14.

107 John Finck, "Clan Leadership in the Hmong Community of Providence, Rhode Island," in *The Hmong in the West: Observations, Reports, Papers of the 1981 Hmong Research Conference, University of Minnesota*. eds. Bruce T. Downing and Douglas P. Olney, (Minneapolis: Southeast Asian Refugee Studies Project, Center for Urban and Regional Affairs, University of Minnesota, 1981), 24; Douglas P. Olney, "We Must Be Organized: Dual Organizations in an American Hmong Community," (Ph.D. diss., University of Minnesota, 1993), 62-63.

108 Finck, in *Hmong in the West*, 25; Olney, 67.

109 "Harassment of Hmong Stirs Concern among Police," *Eau Claire Leader-Telegram*, 15 June 1982; Takaki, 463.

110 "Video is Learning Tool for Hmong," *Eau Claire Leader-Telegram*, 23 January 1989; "Hmong face Housing Bias," *Eau Claire Leader-Telegram*, 21 March, 1993.

111 Roy Beck, "The Ordeal of Immigration in Wausau," *The Atlantic Monthly* 273 (April 1994): 85.

112 Beck, 84-86.

113 Takaki, 465-66.

114 Court Robinson, "Unhappy Endgame: Hmong Refugees in Thailand," *Refugee Reports*, A News Service of the U.S. Committee for Refugees XIII (August 28, 1992): 1-7.

115 "Laotian Rebel Leaders Deported to U.S.," *Agence France Presse*, 21 October 1992.

Selected Annotated Bibliography

Oral Histories

Many of the quotations which appear in the text were excerpted from oral history interviews conducted between 1991 and 1994. The Chippewa Valley Museum, working in cooperation with the Eau Claire Area Hmong Mutual Assistance Association, gathered the stories of Hmong people who had experienced this dramatic journey. A varied group of interviewees — older and younger people, male and female, members of various clans, veterans, USAID employees — offered a range of experiences and viewpoints. Folklorists James Leary and Janet Gilmore interviewed people with special expertise to document particular cultural practices: shamanism, herbalism, needlework, and music. Charles Vue and Kao Xiong had previously interviewed Hmong veterans. A copy of their interviews is on file at the Chippewa Valley Museum. Don Mowry, Social Work Professor at the University of Wisconsin-Eau Claire, contributed transcripts of a series of interviews which he directed for the video, *Creating a Storycloth, Cross-Cultural Interviewing in Social Work Practice: The Case of the Hmong* (1991).

Interviews conducted in English have been reproduced with minimal editing for clarity. When the interviews were conducted in Hmong, we have noted the translator. The interview tapes and transcripts are available for use by researchers at the Chippewa Valley Museum by appointment.

Selected Photographic Sources

Researchers of Hmong culture in Laos and Thailand should visit the National Anthropological Archives (NAA), in the Smithsonian Institution's National Museum of Natural History, as well as the National Geographic Society, in Washington, D.C. Both have extensive collections dating back to the early 1900s. Note that Hmong are sometimes referenced under *Meo* or *Miao*. The strength of the National Geographic collection is the work done by W.E. Garrett in 1973.

Significant private collections include those of Wayne Persons, Terry Wofford, Alfred W. McCoy, and Jan Folsom. Persons worked as a missionary in Laos during the 1960s and early 1970s. His collection is substantial and varied, containing photos that document Hmong culture, missionary activities, the impact of war, and refugee camp life. Freelance photographer Terry Wofford's photos primarily record trips she made to villages in Sayaboury Province in 1968. Historian Alfred W. McCoy visited Laos in August 1971, and owns striking images of rice drops and a funeral ceremony for a Hmong officer. McCoy also possesses a collection of photographs given to him by Touby Lyfoung, dating to the 1950s, relating to the opium trade. Jan Folsom worked with Hmong refugees at Ban Vinai in the 1980s. Her photos document camp life and the refugee craft program.

The best collection of photographs documenting the war in northern Laos and, in particular, the role of Air America, exist in the History of Aviation Collection, Special Collections, McDermott Library, University of Texas at Dallas. Members of the Air America Association, consisting of former pilots, engineers, kickers and other employees, have donated photographs of Long Tieng, Sam Thong, Udorn, and many Lima Sites in northern Laos. The Papers of Lloyd "Pat" Landry include early photos of recruitment and training of Hmong soldiers. The Leslie W. Bays Collection includes identified color photographs and slides, many with explanatory notes by Bays. The Air America collection also includes a substantial number of maps, flight books, records, and correspondence.

Published Sources

Adams, Nina S. and Alfred W. McCoy, eds. *Laos: War and Revolution*. New York: Harper & Row, 1970.

This valuable collection of 30 essays provides a thorough analysis of 20th century Laotian history, divided under five headings: the land and its people, the historical development of modern Laos, America in Laos, United States statements on Laos, and the Pathet Lao. Linguist Noam Chomsky provides an introduction sharply critical of U.S. policy. Alfred W. McCoy contributes an essay on the French colonial administration and the growth of Lao nationalism. Other essayists focus on Air America, the U.S. Agency for International Development, the 1954 Geneva Agreements and Laotian neutrality, the air war and U.S. presidential policies.

Barney, G. Linwood. "The Hmong of Northern Laos." M.A. thesis, University of Minnesota, 1957, in *Indochinese Refugee Education Guides: Glimpses of Hmong History and Culture*. Washington, D.C.: Center for Applied Linguistics, November 1980.

Barney worked as a missionary among the Hmong in northern Laos from 1950 to 1954. He begins with an overview of the many ethnic groups in the region, then describes Hmong social and political organization, subsistence economy, folklore, spiritual beliefs and life cycle. Barney's work is especially valuable because he wrote about Hmong lifeways just before they were seriously disrupted by war.

Beck, Roy. "The Ordeal of Immigration in Wausau." *The Atlantic Monthly* 273 (April 1994): 84-97.

Beck describes the impact of Hmong resettlement on Wausau, a small city in central Wisconsin. He stresses the financial consequences of large numbers of refugees on public assistance and chronicles the divisive battle over school busing which resulted in a school board recall election. Beck also summarizes the evolution of 20th century U.S. immigration policy and highlights the role of federal and voluntary agencies in resettlement.

Bliatout, Bruce Thowpaou, Bruce T. Downing, Judy Lewis, and Dao Yang. *Handbook for Teaching Hmong-Speaking Students.* Folsom, CA: Folsom Cordova Unified School District, Southeast Asia Community Resource Center, 1988.

Classroom teachers of Hmong students should make use of this concise handbook which begins with a historical overview of the Hmong and their journey to the United States and follows with chapters devoted to changing educational experiences, linguistic characteristics of the Hmong language, and recommended instructional and curricular strategies for Hmong language development. The bibliography and extensive appendices recommend further reading materials in Hmong and English, along with suggested individuals and organizations to contact.

Castle, Timothy. *At War in the Shadow of Vietnam: U.S. Military Aid to the Royal Lao Government, 1955-75.* New York: Columbia University Press, 1992.

Castle draws upon a wealth of recently declassified documents and participant interviews to chronicle U.S. covert activities in Laos from 1955 to 1975. His analysis describes how and why U.S. policymakers recruited Laotian minorities for a secret army to advance broader strategic interests in Southeast Asia. Castle provides a detailed account of the military mechanisms used to accomplish American objectives while maintaining the facade of nonintervention. He emphasizes the extraordinary role played by Ambassador William Sullivan in overseeing the deployment of U.S. air power.

Dommen, Arthur J. *Conflict in Laos: The Politics of Neutralization.* New York: Praeger, 1971.

On the scene during the political crises of the late 1950s and early 1960s, Dommen offers a detailed, firsthand description of shifting political alliances and movements which undermined Laotian neutrality. Dommen contends that U.S. interference polarized the political climate and unnecessarily escalated the conflict. The Royal Lao Government remained corrupt and out of touch with the rural population, the majority of Laotian citizens. He witnessed American efforts to buy elections. He notes that, in contrast, the Pathet Lao drew strength by living and working in rural villages.

Donnelly, Nancy D. "The Changing Lives of Refugee Hmong Women." Ph.D. diss., University of Washington, 1989.

Donnelly's thorough study documents and contextualizes the experiences of refugee Hmong women in the Seattle area over nearly a decade. Donnelly describes the realm of Hmong women in Laotian society, and analyzes changes engendered by war, refugee camps, and resettlement to the United States. Extended passages describe

particular cultural practices such as needlework and courtship/marriage customs. This study has recently been revised and published as a book under the same title by the University of Washington Press (1994).

Downing, Bruce T., and Douglas P. Olney, eds. *The Hmong in the West: Observations, Reports, Papers of the 1981 Hmong Research Conference, University of Minnesota.* Minneapolis: Southeast Asian Refugee Studies Project, Center for Urban and Regional Affairs, University of Minnesota, 1981.

The papers of this national conference on Hmong resettlement issues are divided into four chapters focusing on Hmong culture and culture change, language and communication, language learning issues, and problems and prospects in America. Selected essays focus on clan leadership, marriage and birth customs, folklore, New Year celebrations, language structure and acquisition of English, Sudden Death Syndrome, nutrition and employment. Several essays offer case studies of particular Hmong American communities.

Evans, Grant. *The Yellow Rainmakers: Are Chemical Weapons Being Used in Southeast Asia?* London: Verso, 1983.

Distressed by reports of chemical warfare in Laos and dissatisfied by media coverage of the issue, Evans conducted a comprehensive investigation of available scientific data and government reports. He also traveled to Laos and Thailand to interview villagers and refugees on the scene during the alleged attacks. He concluded that the Pathet Lao had used chemical defoliants left behind after the American withdrawal, yet was unable to confirm any attacks of "yellow rain." He found significant holes in the U.S. government's case, and instances where important scientific evidence was lacking. In his interviews with Hmong refugees and villagers, he found numerous inconsistencies that led him to believe that the stories were manufactured. Evans might be accused of being overly sympathetic toward the Pathet Lao government, but his conclusions are well-documented and sound.

Fall, Bernard B., edited with an epilogue by Roger M. Smith. *Anatomy of a Crisis: The Laotian Crisis of 1960-61.* New York: Doubleday, 1969.

On the scene during the period, Fall provides a detailed analysis of political developments from the 1958 elections to the political crisis triggered by the Kong Le coup and transfer of U.S. support to the far right. Fall argues that flawed American policies polarized Laotian politics, undermined the neutralists, and pushed the country unnecessarily to war. Fall also compares European and American media coverage of the events. He accuses the American press of naive and even ignorant coverage which uncritically reported U.S. and Royal Lao government statements, creating harmful misimpressions of the situation.

Fass, Simon M. *The Hmong in Wisconsin: On the Road to Self-Sufficiency.* Milwaukee: The Wisconsin Policy Research Institute Report, April 1991.

Fass discusses the economic challenges faced by Hmong refugees in Wisconsin, and analyzes the effectiveness of existing programs designed to promote self-sufficiency. He chronicles the decreasing fiscal role of the federal government over time, as the states assumed a greater share of the cost of supporting and training refugees. Fass also explains the Key State Initiative, an innovative program which aimed to overcome common barriers by developing plans to fit the unique needs of particular families.

Garrett, W.E. "The Hmong of Laos: No Place to Run." *National Geographic* 145 (January 1974): 78-111.

Garrett examines the impact of years of bombing and warfare on the Hmong at a time of tense, political ambiguity. He offers useful background on the culture of the Hmong and the nature of the conflict, and visits and interviews individual villagers. Striking photographs reinforce his essay by illustrating the rugged, mountainous terrain and the lifeways of a people disrupted by war.

Gettleman, Marvin E., Jane Franklin, Marilyn Young, and H. Bruce Franklin, eds. *Vietnam and America: A Documented History.* New York: Grove Press, Inc., 1985.

The editors use documents, letters, speeches, interviews and other primary sources to allow the conflict's participants to outline the politics of the Vietnam War. A narrative essay begins each section, setting up the documents to follow. Most of the attention is on Vietnam, but early sections include the politics of Laos and the peace accords at Geneva.

Goldfarb, Mace, M.D. *Fighters, Refugees, Immigrants: A Story of the Hmong.* Minneapolis: Carolrhoda Books, Inc., 1982.

Goldfarb volunteered as a doctor at Ban Vinai refugee camp in 1979. His short, highly-illustrated book chronicles his experiences and offers impressions of camp conditions and the character of the people living there. While his sympathy for the Hmong colors the writing, his accounts are straightforward and descriptive, and convey an impression of camp life as surprisingly dynamic.

Gunn, Geoffrey C. *Political Struggles in Laos, 1930-54: Vietnamese Communist Power and the Struggle for National Independence.* Bangkok: Editions Duang Kamol, 1988.

Gunn outlines the political hierarchy, employed by the French to govern Indochina, which allowed a limited amount of autonomy to the Hmong minority. He describes the rise of Touby Lyfoung in the Nong Het region, and his role in support of French guerillas during the Japanese occupation. Gunn also notes the impoverishment of Hmong villagers due to heavy taxation, and the emergence of Lo Faydang as a rebel leader allied with the Vietminh.

Hamilton-Merritt, Jane. *Tragic Mountains: The Hmong, the Americans, and the Secret Wars for Laos, 1942-1992.* Indianapolis: Indiana University Press, 1993.

Hamilton-Merritt interviewed a number of American and Hmong participants for this work focusing on the role of the Hmong in the Southeast Asian wars. The interviews provide interesting details of individual experiences, but the author fails to add appropriate context. Hamilton-Merritt's strong and obvious bias makes *Tragic Mountains* problematic. She romanticizes descriptions of key participants and events, and omits sources which offer alternative perspectives. Since its publication, *Tragic Mountains* has been heatedly debated by scholars of Southeast Asia history. Readers must cross-check her accounts with other published sources.

Hammond, Ruth. "Rumors of War." *Twin Cities Reader* 25-31 October 1989 (Part I): 8-14; 8-14 November 1989 (Part II): 10-20.

Hammond conducted hundreds of interviews to uncover the growing rift within Hmong American communities over whether to support ongoing military resistance in Laos under the leadership of Vang Pao's *Neo Hom*. In Part I, she details the fundraising activities of *Neo Hom*, and articulates the criticism of opponents who either oppose resistance, or question whether funds are being properly accounted for and disbursed. Part II details the role of Lao Family Community, officially a self-help refugee social service organization, as a front for resistance activities. A compressed version of Hammond's research appeared in the *The Washington Post*, 16 April 1989, B1-4.

Hendricks, Glenn L., Bruce T. Downing, and Amos S. Deinard, eds. *The Hmong in Transition.* New York: Centre for Migration Studies, 1986.

This collection of essays is the result of a 1983 research conference at the University of Minnesota. Essays are grouped under four section headings: Hmong culture and change, adapting to a new society, language and literacy, health care issues. Researchers approach the topic from multiple disciplines, examining the social structure, language, and culture of the Hmong in Laos and the consequences of resettlement in the United States.

Hmong Lives: From Laos to La Crosse. Compiled and translated by Wendy Mattison, Laotou Lo, and Thomas Scarseth. La Crosse, Wisconsin: The Pump House Regional Center for the Arts, 1994.

This compilation of interviews with Hmong elders in La Crosse is one result of a three-year collaboration between the Pump House Regional Center for the Arts and the La Crosse Hmong community. The interviews, conducted with Hmong men and women, combine chronicles of life experiences with details about particular cultural practices, such as marriage ceremonies, music, shamanism, and funeral practices. Some of the men interviewed give detailed accounts of their war experiences. The text is printed in Hmong and English.

Hmong Art: Tradition and Change. Sheboygan, Wisconsin: John Michael Kohler Arts Center, 1986.

The Kohler Arts Center organized one of the first exhibits of Hmong art in the United States, bringing together works from around the country. The catalog offers many photographs of textiles, silverwork, musical instruments and agricultural tools, although the emphasis is on needlework. Timothy Dunnigan, Amy Catlin, and Joanne Cubbs contribute scholarly essays which offer historical background, explore Hmong music and language, and examine artistic forms and meanings.

Isaacs, Arnold R., Gordon Hardy, and MacAlister Brown, eds. *Pawns of War: Cambodia and Laos.* Boston: Boston Publishing Co., 1987.

One in the series, *The Vietnam Experience, Pawns of War* provides an introduction to the wars in Cambodia and Laos from 1945 to the 1980s written for the general reader. Numerous contemporary photographs illustrate the land and its people, and introduce readers to the nature of the conflict. Useful maps depict areas of occupation, and the strategic importance of the Ho Chi Minh trail to the larger conflict in Southeast Asia.

Johnson, Charles, and Se Yang, eds. *Myths, Legends and Folk Tales from the Hmong of Laos.* St. Paul: Macalester College, 1985, reprint 1992.

Linguist Charles Johnson and Se Yang, formerly a teacher in Laos, have collected and transcribed nearly 30 Hmong folk tales which appear in Hmong and English. Explanatory notes follow many of the tales and help place characters and events into the context of Hmong culture and spiritual beliefs. The work highlights the importance of oral tradition in understanding Hmong history.

Knoll, Tricia. *Becoming Americans: Asian Sojourners, Immigrants, and Refugees in the Western United States.* Portland, Oregon: Coast to Coast Books, 1982.

Knoll's study of Asian American resettlement to the western United States is divided according to the immigrants' country of origin and includes many groups. In this way, it is perhaps more useful than some case studies of the Hmong because the reader gets a sense of the common hurdles faced by immigrants. Her chapters on the Hmong and other Southeast Asian groups, refugees from the Vietnam War, mix rich personal accounts with a clear contextual framework.

Lamour, Catherine and Michel R. Lamberti. *The International Connection: Opium from Growers to Pushers.* New York: Pantheon Books, 1974.

Part 2 in this study focuses on the Golden Triangle, a rich opium growing area which includes parts of Burma, China, Thailand, Laos, and Vietnam. Chapter 8, "Laos: the Dwindling Kingdom" includes an interview with Touby Lyfoung who describes the opium trade under the French Administration. The authors note that widespread bombing during the war depressed local production, but offer ample evidence that the trade continued.

Lewis, Paul and Elaine. *Peoples of the Golden Triangle: Six Tribes in Thailand.* London: Thames and Hudson, 1984.

In their chapter on the Hmong in Thailand, Paul and Elaine Lewis provide an anthropological overview of lifeways which includes descriptions of clothing and needlework, language, silverwork, village structure, housing, family and clan, courtship and marriage, and spiritual practices. Striking color photographs reinforce their analysis. The book provides a thorough introduction to Hmong culture. Readers should be aware that regional variations distinguish Laotian Hmong from the Hmong in Thailand.

Littauer, Raphael, and Norman Uphoff, eds. *The Air War in Indochina.* Boston: Beacon Press, 1972, rev. ed.

This study evaluates the extensive U.S. bombing campaigns in northern and southern Laos conducted to halt Pathet Lao and North Vietnamese advances into Laos, and to stem the flow of troops and supplies along the Ho Chi Minh trail. In 1969 the number of bombing sorties peaked at over 300 per day. The bombing caused only a temporary disruption of movement along the trail, but in the process created hundreds of thousands of refugees.

Long, Lynnellyn. *Ban Vinai: The Refugee Camp.* New York: Columbia University Press, 1993.

Long's description of camp life at Ban Vinai revolves around the experiences of five households which she interviewed from February through December 1986. She examined the internal workings of camp leadership, economics and social relationships, and noted the cultural mechanisms employed by refugees to cope with camp existence. She described the "refugee consciousness" that the camp created among refugees and relief workers. She also reported the use of Ban Vinai as a staging area for Hmong resistance fighters crossing over into Laos.

McCoy, Alfred W., Cathleen B. Read, and Leonard P. Adams II. *The Politics of Heroin in Southeast Asia.* New York: Harper & Row, 1972.

McCoy offers a comprehensive description of the opium trade during the French administration of Indochina, and subsequent alliance with the Hmong during World War II. His description includes a detailed account of the origins and evolution of the rivalry between Hmong leaders Touby Lyfoung and Lo Faydang. McCoy reports that the opium trade continued with American knowledge during the "Secret War." He follows the trade from the Hmong poppy fields to the heroin production factories, and notes the impact of the war on local villagers. He is sharply critical of General Vang Pao's leadership during the war, and charges him as a participant in the trade. McCoy interviewed leading political and military figures on the scene. McCoy revised and updated this work in *The Politics of Heroin: C.I.A. Complicity in the Global Drug Trade* (Brooklyn: Lawrence Hill Books, 1991)

Miller, Susan Lindbergh, Bounthavy Kiatoukaysy, and Tou Yang, eds. *Hmong Voices in Montana.* Missoula, Montana: Missoula Museum of the Arts Foundation, 1993.

This book grew from an exhibit of the same name detailing the lives and culture of the Hmong residents of Missoula, Montana. The highly illustrated catalog makes good use of oral histories to chronicle historical experiences and cultural practices. The family of deceased CIA operative Jerry Daniels, a Missoula native, made available several striking photographs and personal letters.

Office of Refugee Resettlement, *Hmong Resettlement Study, Volume I, Final Report.* Washington, D.C.: U.S. Department of Health and Human Services, Social Security Administration, April 1985.

This comprehensive study of Hmong resettlement in the United States was a joint undertaking of the Northwest Regional Educational Laboratory (Portland, Oregon), the University of Minnesota, and Lao Family Community (Santa Ana, California). The study provides case studies of numerous communities, and extended narrative explanations discuss how the Hmong are faring in terms of education, employment and self-sufficiency. The study aimed to discover the status of Hmong refugees and assess the effectiveness of existing services. A well-written background essay places Hmong resettlement in its historical and cultural context.

Olney, Douglas P. "We Must Be Organized: Dual Organizations in an American Hmong Community." Ph.D. diss., University of Minnesota, 1993.

Olney describes Hmong mutual assistance associations (MAAs) as "dual organizations." They combine the informal support networks set up by arriving refugees to cope in their new environment, with the characteristics of western nonprofit organizations expected by the host community. Olney sees them as a mechanism for preserving ethnic identity while promoting adaptation and economic independence.

Peterson, Sally. "From the Heart and the Mind: Creating *Paj Ntaub* in the Context of Community." Ph.D. diss., University of Pennsylvania, 1990.

Peterson explores the making and meaning of Hmong *paj ntaub* in changing political and social circumstances. She quotes frequently from Hmong women who speak authoritatively about the role of needlework in daily and celebratory events, the shared and deeply personal meanings of designs, the methods of teaching and learning, and the criteria for competent creation. In the United States, the need to contribute to the family income has engendered significant alterations in needle-work as women modify their work to appeal to Western tastes.

Quincy, Keith. *Hmong: History of a People.* Cheney, Washington: Eastern Washington University Press, 1988.

Quincy's account is one of the first published histories of the Hmong which traced their story from China to the United States. He includes extensive chapters on the Hmong kingdoms in China and their persecution by various Chinese emperors. He outlines agricultural lifeways in Laos and describes spiritual practices and rites of passage. Quincy presents a useful introduction, although he does not cite any of his sources, making it difficult for readers to verify the accuracy of his work.

Ranard, Donald A. "Thailand, The Last Bus." *The Atlantic* (October 1987): 26-34.

The graphic at the beginning of this article depicts a group of refugees perched precariously atop a single domino surrounded by others which have fallen. The image conveys a strong impression, reinforced and detailed by Ranard, of a refugee community which is unsure of its future. Ranard chronicles the dilemma of Hmong at Ban Vinai, facing the fearful choices of returning to Laos or resettling in a strange land.

Robbins, Christopher. *Air America.* New York: G.P. Putnam's Sons, 1979.

Robbins interviewed a number of former Air America pilots, kickers, engineers and other employees for this description of the role of the CIA's airline in support of the war in Laos. Using a journalistic style, Robbins includes numerous pilot anecdotes to describe the hazards of flying presented by jutting mountains, swirling winds, tropical mist and monsoons, and slash and burn agriculture. Robbins wrote about the role of U.S. Air Force pilots in a similar work, *The Ravens: The Men Who Flew in America's Secret War in Laos* (New York: Crown, 1987).

Robinson, Court. "Unhappy Endgame: Hmong Refugees in Thailand." *Refugee Reports,* A News Service of the U.S. Committee for Refugees XIII (August 28, 1992): 1-7.

Robinson reports on a site visit to Laotian refugee camps in Thailand as representatives from cooperating countries pursued a plan to close the camps permanently. Hmong refugees have offered the staunchest resistance to the plan, partially out of fear of forced repatriation to Laos or resettlement to a strange third country, and partially because of the ongoing military resistance which has a stake in keeping the camps open.

Rolland, Barbara J. and Houa Vue Moua. *Trail Through the Mists.* Eau Claire, Wisconsin: By the authors, 1994.

Houa Moua and her husband Kay were one of the first Hmong couples to resettle in Eau Claire in 1976. Barbara Rolland, then a foreign language instructor at the University of Wisconsin - Eau Claire, became involved in developing ESL programs for the growing Hmong community. This collaborative work, based upon interviews conducted over more than a year, details Houa Moua's life as a young girl growing up in war-torn Laos, and traces her experiences up to the decision to flee with her husband. Vivid and often touching descriptions offer an unusual perspective on the daily life of Hmong villagers.

Schanche, Don. *Mister Pop.* New York: David McKay, 1970.

Schanche details the work of Edgar "Pop" Buell, an International Voluntary Service employee who played a leadership role in organizing relief efforts for Hmong and other highlanders displaced by the war. He follows Buell's work from his arrival in the early 1960s through the establishment of refugee headquarters at Sam Thong and Ban Xon. Schanche's account is fictionalized, yet the essential details of his story ring true when compared with scholarly works. Although he sometimes overly romanticizes his subject, Schanche offers an unusual "highland" perspective to the daily events of the war.

Smalley, William A., Chia Koua Vang, and Gnia Yee Yang. *Mother of Writing: The Origin and Development of a Hmong Messianic Script.* Chicago: University of Chicago Press, 1990.

Linguist William Smalley examines the life of Hmong spiritual leader, Shong Lue Yang, and the messianic script that this reportedly uneducated farmer developed in the 1960s. Smalley himself worked to develop a written alphabet for the Hmong in Laos in the 1950s. Chia Koua Vang was one of Shong Lue's leading disciples. *Mother of Writing* provides an overview of Shong Lue's life in the context of Hmong culture and the war, as well as a detailed examination of the script itself. Chia Koua Vang, Gnia Yee Yang and William Smalley authored a related work, *The Life of Shong Lue Yang: Hmong "Mother of Writing,"* (Southeast Asian Refugee Studies, Occasional Papers, Number Nine, 1990) which provides further details of Shong Lue's life and work.

Stuart-Fox, Martin, ed. *Contemporary Laos: Studies in the Politics and Society of the Lao People's Democratic Republic.* St. Lucia: University of Queensland Press, 1982.

This collection of 18 essays examines the first five years of rule by the Lao People's Revolutionary Party. An essay by Hmong scholar Gary Yia Lee describes the position of the Hmong after the American withdrawal in 1975, noting the incident at Hin Heup bridge. Stuart-Fox describes the internal security problems caused by the ongoing Hmong resistance and its implications for relations between Laos and Thailand.

Takaki, Ronald. *Strangers from a Different Shore: A History of Asian Americans.* Boston: Little, Brown and Company, 1989.

Takaki's book provides a scholarly, well-researched discussion of more than a century of Asian immigration to the United States. His description of Hmong refugees, a relatively brief section within a chapter on Southeast Asians, uses quotations from refugees living across the country to convey the significant issues of resettlement.

Trueba, Henry T., Lila Jacobs, and Elizabeth Kirton. *Cultural Conflict and Adaptation: The Case of the Hmong Children in American Society.* New York: The Falmer Press, 1990.

Examining the Hmong community in La Playa, California, this study discusses the alienation and cultural conflicts faced by Hmong school children, and the corresponding challenges for educators. The authors contextualize their analysis by describing the Hmong as a people who have undertaken numerous migrations and experienced generations of "statelessness." They also describe the policy adopted by the U.S. State Department in accepting Hmong for resettlement.

Usowski, Peter S. "Intelligence Estimates and U.S. Policy Toward Laos, 1960-63." *Intelligence and National Security,* 6, 2 (1991): 367-94.

Usowski analyzes the often conflicting advice that President Kennedy received from the State Department, the Joint Chiefs of Staff, and the Central Intelligence Agency as he formulated American policy on Laos at a pivotal point in the conflict's history. Kennedy devoted much of his early presidency toward resolving what had escalated into a politically volatile situation. Usowski's analysis dispels the illusion of a clear, rational method of developing policy, in favor of one which contains multiple personalities and competing agencies and interests.

Wiens, Herold J. *China's March Toward The Tropics.* Hamden, Connecticut: The Shoe String Press, 1954.

Wiens traces the southward penetration of China's culture and peoples in relation to the non-Han-Chinese peoples of South China from his perspective as historian and cultural geographer. In the process, he lays out the migration of the "Miao" across Siberia, Mongolia and Southern China over many centuries. He cites Chinese imperial archives to describe the alternate policies of limited autonomy and armed suppression which characterized Chinese rule over the Miao, later known as the Hmong, and notes their subsequent migration into Southeast Asia. Interestingly, Wiens notes the similarities between the treatment of the Miao by the Han Chinese, and the treatment of native peoples by Euro-Americans.

Xiong, May, and Nancy D. Donnelly. "My Life in Laos." In *Hmong World I,* eds. Brenda Johns and David Strecker, 200-43. New Haven: Yale University, Southeast Asia Studies, 1986.

Xiong participated in a series of life-history interviews conducted by Donnelly who transcribed the tapes, put them into a chronological narrative, and made corrections according to Xiong's suggestions. The story recounts Xiong's life, from her birth in northern Laos in 1952 to her arrival in Thailand in 1977. Xiong's story says much about the experience of women in Laotian Hmong society, with particular regard to marriage rites, birthing, herbalism and shamanism. She also describes two years of living in the jungle following the American 1975 withdrawal. *Hmong World I,* the first and only edition, contains related essays on shamanism, music, marriage rites, and refugee status.

Yang Dao, Ph.D. *Hmong at the Turning Point.* Minneapolis: WorldBridge Associates, Ltd., 1993.

This book is a revised and expanded version of Yang Dao's 1975 work, *Les Hmong du Laos Face au Developpement* (Vientiane: Siaosavath). Yang Dao documents the Hmong agricultural economy and disruptive impact of the war. He gives detailed explanations of the importance of rice, corn, hemp, opium and livestock. An early chapter provides population statistics and background on the Hmong migration into Laos from China. The final chapter outlines the political situation in Laos in 1975 after the American withdrawal.

Yang, Doua and David North. *Profiles of the Highland Lao.* Washington, D.C.: Office of Refugee Resettlement, U.S. Department of Health and Human Services, November 1988.

This study of Hmong in the United States differs from the earlier *Hmong Resettlement Study* (1985) in that it offers less narrative analysis, but provides state by state statistical profiles of Hmong communities. Profiles note population, family size and dominant clan, employment, income status and welfare utilization, and list organizational resources to contact for more information.

Zasloff, Joseph J. and Leonard Unger, eds. *Laos: Beyond the Revolution.* London: Macmillan, 1991.

This book offers a collection of papers presented at a May 1988 conference on contemporary Laos. The essays are grouped according to the topics: Laotian politics, economics, society and external relations, and past and present U.S. policy toward Laos. Wendy Batson reports on the position of ethnic minorities. W. Courtland Robinson examines Laotian refugees in Thailand, and the response of the American and Thai governments to the dilemma of refugee resettlement in Laos. Arthur Dommen's paper, "Lao Nationalism and American Policy 1954-59" is critical of American policy and makes use of recently declassified diplomatic correspondence in the National Archives.

Bibliographies

Boyer, Laura M. *The Older Generation of Southeast Asian Refugees: An Annotated Bibliography.* Minneapolis: Center for Urban and Regional Affairs, Southeast Asian Refugee Studies (SARS) Occasional Papers Number Eleven, University of Minnesota, 1991.

Boyer divides entries according to refugee groups – Cambodian, Ethnic Chinese, Hmong, Lao, Vietnamese, and Southeast Asian (General) – and includes an author and subject index. SARS publishes a quarterly newsletter which tracks the latest scholarship on Southeast Asian refugees, reviews significant works, and announces planned programs and conferences. Scholars who have the opportunity to visit SARS will find a wealth of accessible research materials. SARS newsletters and publications can be ordered by contacting SARS at University of Minnesota, 330 Hubert H. Humphrey Center, 301 19th Avenue South, Minneapolis, MN 55455.

Cordell, Helen, compiler. *Laos.* World Bibliographical Series, Vol. 133, Santa Barbara, CA: CLIO Press, 1991.

This annotated bibliography of Laos includes chapters on geography and geology, archaeology and prehistory, history, population and demography, ethnic groups with a section devoted to the Hmong, economy, government, education, arts, literature, and music. The bulk of the citations on Laotian history deal with the 20th century and the First and Second Indochina Wars. Cordell includes sources from multiple perspectives and notes perceived author biases. Later chapters direct readers to news sources, periodicals, directories, and archival resources.

Dalley, George. *Books on Southeast Asia and the Indochina Wars.* Christiansburg, Virginia: Dalley Book Service, March 1994.

This catalog offered by the Dalley Book Service has 2,150 entries of published and unpublished sources, most focusing on the Indochina Wars, divided according to the following headings: Vietnam fiction and nonfiction, Cambodia, Laos, Thailand, Southeast Asia: history and politics, OSS, CIA & Intelligence, and Guerilla Warfare. Most entries are briefly annotated, and Dalley continually updates it.

Olney, Douglas P., comp. *A Bibliography of the Hmong (Miao) of Southeast Asia and the Hmong Refugees in the United States,* 2nd ed. Minneapolis: Center for Urban and Regional Affairs, Southeast Asian Refugee Studies (SARS) Occasional Papers Number One, University of Minnesota, 1983.

Olney provides broad coverage of available resources on the Hmong, dividing entries under the headings: General works, Hmong ethnography in Asia and the United States, linguistic studies, resettlement issues, physical and mental health, journalism, Hmong language books, bibliographies, films and videos, and introductory reading.

Smith, J. Christina, comp. *The Hmong: An Annotated Bibliography, 1983-87.* Minneapolis: Center for Urban and Regional Affairs, Southeast Asian Refugee Studies (SARS) Occasional Papers Number Seven, University of Minnesota, 1988.

Smith lists entries under the broad headings: bibliographies, ethnography, linguistics, refugee/resettlement issues, physical and mental health, bilingual materials, audiovisual materials, sources and an author's index. In contrast to Cordell's work, this bibliography emphasizes resettlement issues.

About the Chippewa Valley Museum

The Chippewa Valley Museum in Eau Claire, Wisconsin, presents the history of the Chippewa Valley, from the time of its earliest inhabitants some 10,000 years ago to the present day. Opened in 1974 by area residents committed to preserving and interpreting regional heritage, the museum operates as a professional institution strongly based in its community. The Chippewa Valley Museum was accredited by the American Association of Museums in 1987.

Major long-term exhibits include *Settlement and Survival: Building Towns in the Chippewa Valley, 1850-1925; Paths of the People: the Ojibwe in the Chippewa Valley*; and *Rural Heritage*. Regional experience provides a perspective from which to consider not only what is unique in this region of Northwestern Wisconsin but how events, issues and conditions shape American life. As a result, CVM engages the interest of visitors from throughout the United States as well as the active involvement of local residents. Many students "experience" history in the Sunnyview School or Anderson Log House, located on the museum grounds, or in exhibit-based programs tied to the curriculum goals of area schools. Short-term exhibits, seminars, workshops and special events are scheduled throughout the year. The lively CVM program results from the efforts of its professional staff of 11, more than 300 active volunteers and the on-going financial support of 1,900 members, the City and County of Eau Claire, and the Chippewa Valley Museum Foundation. CVM has been recognized on state and national levels for its exhibits, collections care, and publications.

In 1991, CVM and the Eau Claire Area Hmong Mutual Assistance Association (HMAA) began a cooperative project to document the experiences of the Eau Claire Hmong community, build a permanent folk arts collection for HMAA, and expand public programming on Hmong history and culture. The exhibit, *Hmong in Eau Claire: Refugees from a Secret War* (October 1993 - June 1994), an extensive oral history project, and the reading discussion series, *Journey from the Plain of Jars,* resulted from this collaboration. Activities in Eau Claire became the model for a national project, *Hmong in America,* which began in 1994. The National Endowment for the Humanities provided a major grant to present panel exhibits and the *Journey from the Plain of Jars* series in five other cities with significant Hmong populations: Charlotte, North Carolina; La Crosse, Wisconsin; Sacramento, California; Minneapolis/St. Paul, Minnesota; and Seattle, Washington. Central to the research and planning of the project was the works of scholars on various aspects of Hmong history and culture and the personal accounts of Hmong people who have lived this dramatic story.

The Chippewa Valley Museum, located in Eau Claire's Carson Park, is open year round, Tuesday through Sunday, 1-5 p.m., with extended summer hours. For more information about exhibits, programs or publications, contact: Chippewa Valley Museum, P.O. Box 1204, Eau Claire WI 54702, (715) 834-7871.

Index

Acknowledgments

Major funding

Hmong in America
National Endowment for the Humanities

Hmong in Eau Claire
National Endowment for the Arts

Wisconsin Humanities Committee
acting on behalf of the National Endowment for the Humanities

Wisconsin Arts Board
with funds from the State of Wisconsin

Dayton's Community Giving

Members and supporters of the Chippewa Valley Museum
and the Eau Claire Area Hmong Mutual Assistance Association

Academic Consultants

Bruce Downing, Ph.D., *Linguistics, University of Minnesota*; Janet Gilmore, Ph.D., *Wisconsin Folk Museum*; James Leary, Ph.D., *Wisconsin Folk Museum*, Charles Lee, Ph.D., *History Department, University of Wisconsin - La Crosse*, Alfred W. McCoy, Ph.D., *History Department, University of Wisconsin - Madison*, Elizabeth Quinn Owen (Perkins), *Textile Specialist, Writer and Consultant*; Cliff Sloane, *Ethnomusicologist;* Melissa Ringheim Stoddart, *Anthropologist, Science Museum of Minnesota.*

Eau Claire Community Advisors

Neng Lor Lee, Nhia Houa Lor, Yong Kay Moua, Pa Neng Vang, Chia Koua Xiong, Joe Bee Xiong, Cher Xiong Yang.

Chippewa Valley Museum

Brenda Bennett, *design assistant;* Amy Benson, *volunteer coordinator;* Kevin Dallas, *construction supervisor;* Susan Glenz, *education coordinator;* Kevin Graeme, *design intern*; Dondi Hayden, *exhibit technician;* Julie Johnson, *curator of collections;* Susan McLeod, *director;* Jeanne Nyre, *designer;* Tim Pfaff, *curator of public programs;* Judy St. Arnault, *office manager;* Diane Schmidt, *senior curator;* David Tank, *marketing;* Eldbjorg Tobin, *librarian;* Kao Xiong, *Hmong in America project assistant;* Pao Lee, Touly Xiong, and Long Xiong, *interns.*

Eau Claire Area Hmong Mutual Assistance Association

Chou Lee, *executive director*; Joyce Metzgar, *assistant director (planning phase)*; Deanna Smugala, *assistant director*; Chou Va Vue, *elderly aide*; Kao Xiong, *translation services*; Smidchei Xiong, *project coordinator*; Houa Yang, *case manager.*

Oral History Sources

Chong Cha Her; Tang Kue; Neng Lor Lee; Kha Vang Lor; Nhia Houa Lor; Xia Ying Lor; Houa Vue Moua; Song Yai Moua; Xong Chai Moua; Yong Kay Moua; Bao Vang; Mai Moua Vang; Neng Mai Vang; Xia Vang; Chia Koua Xiong; Doua Xiong; Joe Bee Xiong; Kao Xiong; Xia Fong Xiong; Smidchei Xiong; Touly Xiong; Mai Xao Yang.

Translators

Pao Lee, Kao Xiong, Smidchei Xiong, Touly Xiong.

Publication Reviewers

Timothy Castle, Ph.D.; Nancy Dorelle Donnelly, Ph.D.; Bruce Downing, Ph.D.; Susan Hogue; Alfred W. McCoy, Ph.D.; Gayle Morrison; Yong Kay Moua; Elizabeth Quinn Owen (Perkins); Susan Sausker; Melissa Ringheim Stoddart; Kao Xiong.

Services

Carto-Graphics; Eau Claire Press Company Commercial Printing; Johnson Photography; Southeast Asian Refugee Studies, Center for Urban and Regional Affairs, University of Minnesota.

Cover identifications

Front left: **Tou Lee holding son Yia** *inside the family's Eau Claire apartment, August 1987. Photographer: Neal Menschel, ©The Christian Science Monitor. The Lee family had recently resettled in Wisconsin after completing a six-week refugee orientation course at Phanon Nikhom, Thailand. Front right:* **Hmong boy behind barbed wire at a refugee settlement** *at Muong Soui in northern Laos, 1970. Dan Williams.*

Back cover: **Bound for resettlement***, a Hmong woman says a tearful good-bye from a bus at Ban Vinai Refugee Camp, Thailand, ca. 1983-85. Photographer: Jan Folsom.*